Free Them All!

Stories of Chicago's Black and Brown
Torture Survivors, Vol. 1

Chicago Alliance Against Racist
and Political Repression

Dedicated to

Stan Willis and Vickie Casanova

And to the Heroic Survivors of Police Torture and Their Families

And to the memory of

Sylvia Woods, Josephine Wyatt, and Clarice Durham

Cover photographs: Bob Simpson

ISBN: 978-0-359-90322-1

Contents

Torture Survivors

 **Harvey Allen**
page 6

 **James Gibson**
page 26

 **Ivan Smith**
page 44

 **Robert Allen**
page 9

 **Anthony Jakes**
page 30

 **Robert Smith**
page 48

 **George Anderson**
page 13

 **Jerome Johnson**
page 32

 **Sean Tyler**
page 52

 **Tony Anderson**
page 15

 **Scott Mitchell**
page 34

 **Vincent Wade**
page 55

 **Darryl Christian**
page 17

 **Kevin Murray**
page 36

 **Shawn Whirl**
page 57

 **Javan Deloney**
page 20

 **David Randle**
page 38

 **Marcus Wiggins**
page 60

 **Nick Escamilla**
page 22

 **Gerald Reed**
page 41

 **Jackie Wilson**
page 65

 **Darrell Fair**
page 24

 **Clayborn Smith**
page 42

Introduction

Imagine you're driving down the road in your car and you are stopped by the police. They take you to a police station and place you in a room and begin questioning you about crimes you've never heard of. They say the names of people you don't know, claiming you're responsible for killing them. You're confused because you were just coming home from school or your girlfriend's house or work or wherever. You know nothing of what they are saying. They then begin pulling your hair. They may chain you to a desk or a radiator. They start kicking your back, your stomach and head. After the kicking they bring out an electrical box and start shocking your ears, hands, thighs. You plead for a lawyer. So, the police leave you for hours, denying you food, water, and access to a bathroom. They come back, and the beating continues for more hours. Finally, they say you can leave, but only if you sign a piece of paper that they may not even let you read. You sign it because you are so tired, hungry, in pain, and you just want to go home.

> **TORTURE: the action of inflicting severe pain on someone as a punishment or to force a living being to do or say something.**

The story above seems like something made up or something you would see in a movie, and most certainly doesn't seem like something that could happen in your community at the hands of your local police. But, sadly, that has been the harsh reality for hundreds of individuals in Chicago. Chicago has a long history of torture, police violence, and cover-ups by police officers that dates back to the 1960s. The murders of Fred Hampton and Mark Clark in 1969 were a notorious example of the brazenness of police brutality in Chicago (Gregory, 2018), as was the 1968 command of Mayor Richard J. Daley to the Chicago Police to shoot to maim and shoot to kill "looters" in the aftermath of Dr. Martin Luther King's assassination (Chandler, 2002).

While countless detectives and officers continue to perpetrate these atrocities, the best known and documented era of Chicago torture was under the watch of one police commander, Jon Burge. Burge got his start as a military police interrogator in Vietnam. Upon his return to Chicago, he was assigned to the South Side in 1972. Burge led a group of men in police Areas 2 and 3, dubbed the "Chicago Midnight Crew," who were known to use torture to elicit confessions (Sterbenz, 2015). Among the detectives who worked under Burge were Michael Kill, Kenneth Boudreau, John Halloran, James O'Brien, Joseph Stehlik, and Tony Maslanka. Between 1972 and 1981, Burge and his men are known to have tortured over 100 African-Americans into confessions through beatings, suffocation with plastic bags, electrical shocks, and starvation (Berlatsky, 2014).

Burge trained numerous torturers, but there are many others who were "self-taught" and did not work with Burge. Among these were Reynaldo Guevara, who used torture to frame at least 51 individuals, and Richard Zuley, who used interrogation methods similar to the ones he used in Guantanamo Bay to elicit murder confessions from people of color (Ackerman, 2015).

Burge has been the focus of public attention due to his high-profile case, but we cannot ignore the fact that Chicago's history of torture goes beyond one individual and his trainees. This targeted torture has been pervasive and has had a huge impact on the communities which experienced it. Chicago has rightly earned the title: "Torture Capital of the World" (Taylor, 2013).

For years, these false confessions were used to make convictions. The torture was covered up and ignored by then-State's Attorney Richard M. Daley and then-Governor George Ryan. The police department worked hard to ensure that this would never be exposed, while neighborhoods continued to experience the devastation caused by the police as men were being tortured and taken off to prison to serve life sentences.

Burge and the Midnight Crew were finally exposed in the Andrew Wilson case. Andrew Wilson was arrested for killing two police officers. During the interrogation, he endured beatings and torture for hours to force a confession. There were clear, overwhelming, objective medical reports on his injuries. [Andrew's co-defendant and brother, Jackie Wilson, is included in this booklet with more background information on the specifics of their case.]

Activists and torture survivors began to share their stories and make the issue public in the media, the courts, and the international community. In 2001, Governor George Ryan pardoned four men tortured by Burge and commuted the death sentences of many others. Ryan eventually placed a moratorium on the death penalty in Illinois, based upon multiple cases that had been overturned by DNA evidence (Tribune Staff Reports, 2003).

Between 2002 and 2006, Special Prosecutor Edward Egan investigated allegations of torture made by individuals who were pardoned or freed on the basis of DNA evidence. He concluded that Burge and officers under his command had likely committed torture. In 2008, the U.S. Attorney brought a federal indictment, charging Jon Burge with perjury because he had lied under oath by denying he had tortured anyone. He was not prosecuted for the torture itself due to concerns over the statute of limitations. Burge served less than four years in prison and continued to receive his Chicago Police Department pension (Associated Press, 2016). A majority of the torture survivors remain in prison, serving long sentences for crimes they did not commit, suffering through a long tangle of legal red tape despite their exoneration. As long as they are behind bars, their torture and the agonizing wait of their families and community continue.

On May 6, 2015, the Chicago City Council passed historic legislation that provides reparations to the survivors of police torture in Chicago, making it the only city in the United States that has ever passed legislation of this kind. The legislation provides: 1) a pool of $20 million to the survivors; 2) funding for the Chicago Torture Justice Center which provides services to individuals who have experienced trauma due to police violence; and 3) for a mandatory curriculum focused on teaching about Burge's abuses in Chicago Public Schools (Associated Press, 2016).

While there are over 200 individual cases of torture in Chicago, this booklet focuses on 22 cases. All cases matter, and all stories deserve to be told, but we are presenting those cases with enough available documentation at this point. Our goal is for all individuals who went through such a horrific experience to be granted justice, not just those who are highlighted in this booklet. These 22 individual cases have all been reviewed by the Illinois Torture Inquiry and Relief Commission. This is the first installment of this work. These cases will also be featured on our website: www.caarpr.org, and www.StopPoliceCrimes.org. New fact sheets on cases will be added going forward.

The Illinois Torture Inquiry and Relief Commission (Torture Commission) is a state agency created by legislation and signed into law in 2009 following the series of allegations that confessions had been coerced by detectives under the command of Jon Burge. It was passed as a result of mass pressure, especially by Black People Against Police Torture, whose President, Attorney Standish Willis, played an instrumental role in drafting the measure. Following the release of Special Prosecutor Egan's report, efforts were intensified to provide new hearings for individuals who claimed torture by Burge and those under his command.

The Commission works to gather evidence about a claim of torture and then determines whether there is sufficient, credible evidence of torture to merit a judicial review. Cases referred to the courts for review by the Commission are assigned to a Special Prosecutor. It is hopeful that each of these individuals gets a new case, but these special prosecutors often act more as defense attorneys for the police who committed torture rather than as truth-seekers in these cases. While the Commission was originally only authorized to hear claims involving Jon Burge, in 2016, it was allowed to investigate any claims of torture in Cook County.

Twenty of the 22 individual cases described in this booklet have been reviewed by the Torture Commission, and they have found sufficient evidence to warrant a new hearing for each of these survivors.

Of the 22 survivors of torture, 17 were under the age of 25, and 6 were younger than 18 at the time of their arrest and torture. Seventeen of these cases happened in Areas 2 and 3, both located on Chicago's South Side, involving detectives under the command of Burge. All 22 survivors are African American or Latinx. All of them are sons. All of them were community members. None deserved to be tortured.

As a majority of these men lived on the South Side of Chicago, we begin to see the impact on families, communities, and neighborhoods. Countless jobs were lost. Children have grown up with an incarcerated parent. One of the torture survivors, Darrell Fair, was a student attending Roosevelt University at the time of his arrest. Some had wives and children. They all had friends, aspirations, and goals – all torn away when they were tortured and imprisoned.

Collectively, these 22 men have spent a total of 563 years behind bars. These represent 563 years that could have been spent contributing to society, but instead 563 years were taken from them all. This is a huge loss for each of their families and the communities in which they lived. The impact will become apparent as you read the individual stories. One of the survivors, Nick Escamilla, was able to write his own story. You will also read stories from three mothers who express how this has impacted them and their communities.

While a majority of these cases are heart-wrenching and tragic, there are a few success stories. Anthony Jakes and Shawn Whirl have been released and exonerated due to judicial recognition of the torture and wrongful convictions they have endured. We include their stories to highlight some of the successes of the people's movement for justice and to inspire continued pressure for future exonerations and releases. We hope to add more to this list.

Kim Foxx, Cook County State's Attorney, has released 36 individuals from prison, and exonerated 18. Most of the individuals who have been released were not torture survivors, but victims of frame-ups by police officers who are now serving prison time for their corrupt practices (Moore, 2016). These recent exonerations have begun to bring hope and justice to these individuals, but we demand that more be done. We demand that the Governor pardon all the torture survivors, immediately.

The Chicago Alliance Against Racist and Political Repression will continue to actively work on these cases, attending court and Torture Commission hearings and staying involved with family members. We will continue to work on more fact sheets and will put these on our websites, caarpr.org and StopPoliceCrimes.org, as they become available. If you are moved by these stories and would like to find out how to help, contact The Chicago Alliance Against Racist and Political Repression by phone at 312-939-2750.

Source Material:

Ackerman, S. (2015, February 18). Guantanamo torturer led brutal Chicago regime of shackling and confession. *The Guardian.* Retrieved from https://www.theguardian.com

Associated Press. (2016, January 5). Chicago pays $5.5M in reparations to police torture survivors. *NY Daily News.* Retrieved from http://www.nydailynews.com

Berlatsky, N. (2014, December 14). When Chicago tortured. *The Atlantic.* Retrieved from https://www.theatlantic.com

Chandler, C. (2002, April 4). Shoot to maim...shoot to kill. *Chicago Reader.* Retrieved from https://www.chicagoreader.com

Gregory, T. (2018). The Black Panther Raid and the death of Fred Hampton. *The Chicago Tribune.* Retrieved from http://www.chicagotribune.com

Moore, M. (2016, January 6). Victims of Chicago police torture paid reparations years later. *National Public Radio.* Retrieved from https://www.npr.org

Sterbenz, C. (2015, May 6). A group of rogue cops known as the 'Midnight Crew' tortured dozens of people for decades- and now Chicago is paying millions for it. *Business Insider.* Retrieved from http://www.businessinsider.com

Taylor, F. (2013, February 20). Racism, torture, and impunity in Chicago. *The Nation.* Retrieved from https://www.thenation.com

Tribune Staff Reports. (2003, January 10). Ryan pardons 4. *Chicago Tribune.* Retrieved from http://www.chicagotribune.com

Torture Survivors

Harvey Allen

On December 7, 1985, a fire started on the third floor in an apartment building at 1575 E. 70th Street. The victims were Ora Johnson, age 29, her two sons Anthony, age 10, and Willie Tabb, age 11, and their grandmother, Marguerite Stafford, age 51. They were in their third-floor apartment and were killed when a fire (suspected arson) burned through their building.

Within 24 hours, the police had a suspect in custody: Harvey Allen, 35 years old. The prosecution alleged that Harvey Allen was at 1575 E. 70th St. on the evening of December 7, 1985, to purchase narcotics from Sherman Young at his second-floor apartment. According to prosecutors, Allen purchased the narcotics, and then returned home to wait for the delivery. When the narcotics did not arrive, Allen called Young's girlfriend, Sarah Davis, who was at the house. He demanded delivery and threatened to harm Young if he did not show up with the drugs. All of this allegedly happened between the hours of 11:30 pm on December 6, 1985 and 4:30 am on December 7, 1985.

That same night, between 1:30 and 3:00 am, the night manager at a local gas station, Howard Borden, said he saw Allen come to the station and fill up an empty Black Flag Insecticide can with gasoline. The night manager claimed Allen was a friend from the neighborhood, and after he saw Allen fill up the can with gasoline, Allen walked back toward Young's apartment. Borden picked Allen out of a photo array and identified the jacket he was wearing that night. Borden testified to all of this during the trial. The prosecution alleges that the gas insecticide can contained the accelerant to light the fire outside the door of Young's apartment, which tragically killed the family living upstairs.

After the fire on the morning of December 7, 1985, Harvey Allen was arrested at his apartment by four police officers, Detectives James Swistowicz, George Carey, Richard Popovits, and Leo Wilcosz. According to his testimony, he was not advised of his Miranda rights at this time. He was taken to Area 1, a third district Police Station at 51st and Wentworth, where he was interrogated. Around noon, he was moved to the Chicago Police Department at 11th and State St. (in Area 3) by Dets. Carey & Switowicz, where he took a polygraph test that proved inconclusive. The detectives then transported him back to 51st and Wentworth, where his interrogation continued. At this point, he was formally arrested and read his Miranda rights by Det. Anthony Lowrey and Det. Robert Fields. Later that evening, Det. Guy Habiak and his partner, Det. Coffman brought Allen back to his apartment, under the guise of "searching for evidence." There they met Detectives Glynn and Regan. It was unusual to have brought Allen, who was now an arrested suspect, back to his own apartment during their search. Allen testified that they twisted his arms behind his back and dragged him up and down the stairs of his building, in an attempt to get him to confess.

After the torture at his apartment, police brought Allen back to the Area 1 Police Headquarters where he was left in an interrogation room all night without food. On December 8, Allen was still in the interrogation room, and it wasn't until late in the afternoon that a homicide detective brought him a hamburger. Allen had gone over 36 hours without food. An unnamed detective repeatedly told Allen that if he did not confess he would get the death penalty and that Allen should just confess to the fire and say that he did not mean to kill anyone. It was then that Allen asked for his lawyer, and the detective responded by kicking Allen and then moving him into another interrogation room and continuing the interrogation there. Allen again was kept in this room all night and was not allowed to use the bathroom.

On December 9 at 3 a.m., multiple officers entered the room and continued to question Allen. Allen again asked for his lawyer, but the detectives continued to interrogate him, ignoring his constitutional right to counsel. After these police officers left the room, one police officer re-entered and physically abused Allen by kicking him in the groin. He threatened Allen by holding a sharp object to his throat. Det. Popovits told him to confess to make it easy on himself. Det. Popovits brought two other detectives into the interrogation room, and coached Allen on what to say for his confession. Allen says in a sworn affidavit that out of fear for his life he repeated what the detectives told him to say. Later that morning, Assistant State's Attorney (ASA) James Kogut came to speak to Allen. He told Allen that he would not get the death penalty if he confessed to the fire. Allen then explained that Det. Switowicz said that the Assistant State's Attorney would make a deal with Allen for 6 years in a state penitentiary in exchange for his confession. However, Kogut stated that he was not going to issue a deal for Allen, nor was he interested in Allen's explanation of the abuse he suffered at the hands of detectives. Allen continued to ask for his lawyers, but the interrogation continued illegally. After almost two days of abuse with little to no sleep, food, or water, Allen made an oral confession.

At trial, in 1993, the defense noted that there were no eyewitnesses to the crime who could place Allen at the apartment building at the time it caught fire. There was no DNA evidence and, in fact, the jacket Allen was wearing (according to Howard Borden) tested negative for any kind of chemical accelerant, including gasoline. This is in direct contradiction to the testimony of the arson investigator who claimed that the gasoline that started the fire would have had to be splashed all over the apartment door and stairs. It is nearly impossible that Allen would have been able to splash the amount of gasoline needed to start that kind of apartment fire, without getting any gasoline on his clothing. Furthermore, Allen had an alibi: He was at home styling a friend's hair on the night of the fire, then drank some liquor, and went to sleep. Allen did testify that he bought a small amount of gasoline in a Black Flag Insecticide can to fill up his car, which had run out of gas down the road from the station. Allen also maintained that he did not know anything about the fire or the alleged threatening phone calls.

Before the trial began, Allen and his defense attorney filed a motion to suppress his confession through a motion to quash his arrest based on lack of probable cause. Ultimately this suppression was denied due to Allen's attorney choosing to question Allen on the arrest and not questioning him regarding the police abuse. Allen has always maintained that he experienced police abuse, which is consistent with the fact that the prosecution's case against Allen was not strong, and thus needed a confession in order to prosecute. Allen was convicted in a jury trial and sentenced to concurrent terms of seven years and natural life imprisonment for the arson and murder charges respectively.

Allen has filed numerous appeals and petitions in the past years, citing ineffective trial counsel, unreasonable assistance of appellate counsel, and a physically-coerced confession. All of these were denied until Edward Egan came onto the scene. Special State's Attorney Edward Egan was overseeing the cases of police abuse perpetrated by Jon Burge and his men in Areas 2 and 3. When he saw Allen's case, he put forth a petition that Allen was physically abused while staying at an Area 3 police station, and it was due to this abuse that Allen was forced to submit a false confession. Without this confession, there would only have been circumstantial evidence: Borden testifying to seeing Allen walk towards the apartment building the evening of the fire, and Young's girlfriend claiming to have received threatening calls from Allen. Without this coerced confession, it is believed that Allen would never have been convicted.

As of November 2016, the referral from the TIRC, which led to Allen's most recent petition, was rejected by the courts because Allen's case did not involve Jon Burge and his associates. The case was remanded from the Illinois Supreme Court to local circuit courts. Then the TIRC expanded its purview to include non-Jon Burge cases. Allen's case is now able to be reheard, although the date of a future hearing has not been set. Currently, Harvey Allen is incarcerated at the Pontiac Correctional Center.

Robert Allen

Reginald Braggs, a.k.a. Robert Allen, was tortured by Chicago Police Detectives and convicted of three armed robberies and attempted murder based on the detectives' testimony, inconsistent testimony by witnesses, and a coerced confession given by a friend who was also tortured. He was sentenced to a total of 125 years in prison, some concurrent. Robert Allen has been wrongfully imprisoned since 1990. His expected discharge date is 2055.

Torture and frame-up

On April 18, 1990, Robert Allen received a ride to a store at 51st and Aberdeen from Tony Anderson, his friend, and Anderson's girlfriend, Fernice Barkley. Unknown to Allen, the vehicle was stolen. When they left the store on the 5100 block of South Aberdeen and returned to the car, an unmarked police car blocked their car in. Three Chicago Police detectives in plain clothes exited the unmarked police vehicle and approached the car.

According to Detective Patrick Brosman, the car driven by Anderson had drawn the attention of him and his partners, Detectives Welch [first name unknown] and Gregory Seller. It was a beige 1985 Oldsmobile vehicle that they said had passed them at an excessive speed, making a sharp right turn off 53rd street onto Aberdeen. The detectives followed the car north on Aberdeen, passed it, and stopped in front of the store on the corner of 51st St. Detective Brosman ran a license plate check on the vehicle, which revealed that the car had been stolen. The detectives turned around and waited for the occupants to return to the car before blocking the car to prevent it from pulling off.

Detectives Welch and Seller said they approached the driver's side and asked Anderson to roll down the window. Anderson complied, and Seller reached into the vehicle and snatched keys from the ignition, at which point a struggled ensued between Anderson and the two detectives. Ultimately, the detectives pulled Anderson out of the car and handcuffed him.

Detective Brosman said that as Detectives Welch and Seller struggled with Anderson, he approached the passenger side of the car and asked Barkley, who was in the front seat, and Allen, who was in the back seat, to exit the vehicle. Brosman says he opened the passenger side door and told Allen and Barkley that the car was stolen. Brosman testified that because Barkley was very pregnant and he saw Sellers and Welch struggling with Anderson, he told her to stay in the car and to push her seat forward. He said that he then began a pat-down search of Allen, who was still in the rear passenger seat. Brosman admitted the search of Allen was improper, but he did it that way out of consideration for the pregnant

Barkley. Brosman testified that as he completed the search of Allen he saw a black jacket on the floor partially under the front passenger seat. He said he removed the jacket and searched it, discovering a gun in the pocket of the jacket. According to Brosman, upon discovering the gun, the detectives placed Allen and Anderson under arrest. They released Fernice Barkley at the scene without charges.

According to Allen, however, when Brosman approached the passenger side of the vehicle he told Barkley to roll down her window, and he informed both him and Barkley that the vehicle was stolen and asked that they both exit the vehicle, which they did. Brosman did a pat-down of Allen, handcuffed him, and told him to sit on the ground near the store. Allen says that Brosman then went back to the car and searched it. Brosman came back to Allen with a jacket and a handgun that he said he had retrieved from under the front passenger seat. He and Anderson were then placed under arrest and taken to Area 1 Police Headquarters at 11th and State, several miles away. He insists he was never "read his [Miranda] rights."

Robert Allen was initially charged with Criminal Trespass of a Stolen Vehicle and Tony Anderson was charged with Auto Theft. They were informed that they were being taken to 11th and State (Area 1) instead of the closer 51st and Wentworth Police station, which was the location of the Auto Theft Unit. Allen and Anderson were later moved from Area 1 to Area 2 Police Headquarters on the far South Side. They were not told why they were being transferred.

At Area 2 Headquarters, Allen and Anderson were both questioned by Detective Michael McDermott and Detective Anthony Maslanka. Both detectives have been implicated in dozens of cases of torture, and McDermott has admitted under oath that he tortured suspects. They interrogated Anderson and Allen about a series of armed robberies and other crimes unrelated to their initial arrest. McDermott and Maslanka threatened and beat them over the next two days, demanding that they confess to the crimes. Despite two days of repeated torture Allen insisted on his innocence and his lack of knowledge of the robberies and other crimes between March and April 1990 of which he was being accused.

Anderson has claimed that McDermott placed a gun to his head and threatened to "blow his damn brains out" if he did not confess. Maslanka struck him in the chest, ribs, and back with his nightstick. Anderson estimates he was hit over 12 times. To stop this abuse he finally agreed to sign a confession and to also incriminate Robert Allen and another individual, Leo Hicks, in multiple armed robberies. Leo Hicks was never charged, however, with any of these crimes. It was discovered that Anderson had lied under torture because Hicks had been attending a work release program at the times of the crimes.

After Anderson confessed and implicated Allen, they were placed in several lineups. Allen was placed in three different lineups for the purpose of identifying a suspect for three different robberies prior to their arrest: Trak Auto, Robbins Drug Store, and Joyeria Nathaly Jewelry Store. Detective McDermott conducted each lineup.

Allen had three separate trials for robberies at these three different locations.

At Allen's trial for the robbery of the Robbins Drug Store, LaLit Chheda identified Allen in court, but he testified that the prosecutors showed him Allen's line-up photo just before taking the stand. He testified that during the robbery there was a short man and a tall man. He then testified that he was only able to identify Tony Anderson as the short man. He was not sure about the tall man. He also testified that he couldn't remember what type of gun they had used.

Regarding the robbery of the Joyeria Nathaly Jewelry Store, Jose Pulido, the store owner, testified that he saw 3 offenders enter the store, one at a time, but he did not identify Robert Allen. Though he testified that he remembered Allen's face, he was unable to recall anything about his body, his head or hair style, and no facial features were described. Mario Cisneros testified that he had been shown a photo of Robert Allen by Detective Palandino before the line-up. The photo was not part of a display of multiple photos. He was then asked if he could identify the robber in the lineup.

Juan Navarrez testified that he only saw one offender's shoes and red pants. However, he identified Allen in the lineup and in court. Allen was the only person in the lineup wearing red jogging pants.

All three witnesses identified Robert Allen in a lineup in which he was the only person wearing red jogging pants. All three had been shown a photo of Robert Allen by Detectives McDermott and Maslanka prior to the line-up.

In the Trak Auto robbery case, Scott Volk, the assistant manager, testified that he was approached by two men who asked him for help finding some items. He then directed them to where the items were located. The taller man of the two stepped up behind him and placed a gun to the back of his neck. Volk then said he wasn't going to take it anymore, turned his head and was shot. Volk was able to identify the clothing of the men. However, he did not get a good look at their faces. Volk was only able to identify Tony Anderson as the offender after viewing police photographs. However, at Robert Allen's trial, when prompted by the State's Attorney, Volk identified Robert Allen as one of the men who robbed Trak Auto.

Initially, one of two witnesses to the Trak Auto robbery, Ricky Norwood, had been unable to positively identify Robert Allen. However, at Robert Allen's trial, when also prompted by the State's Attorney, Norwood identified Robert Allen as one of the men who robbed Trak Auto.

Of two witnesses to the Robbins Drug Store robbery, one was unable to identify Allen. Also, it must be noted that in the Robbins Drug Store robbery, another individual by the name of Joe Williams was picked out of the lineup and identified as the offender. Joe Williams was never charged in the Robbins Drug Store robbery. [Update: Tony Anderson is the a.k.a. for Joe Williams. Joe Williams a.k.a. Tony Anderson was in fact charged and convicted of the Robbins Drug Store robbery.]

Three witnesses in the Joyeria Nathaly Jewelry Store robbery identified Allen only because he was the one person in the line-up wearing red jogging pants, and the robber had also worn red jogging pants.

Allen was tried for each robbery separately. The handgun discovered during his initial arrest was introduced at each trial as the weapon used to commit each crime, although there was no forensic or material evidence tying the gun to any of the crimes. There was no evidence linking Allen to the gun found in the car. The gun had neither Allen's nor Anderson's fingerprints. Allen's Aunt and Uncle, Mr. and Mrs. Williams testified on his behalf. Mr. Williams is also the biological uncle of Tony Anderson.

Given that Allen did not confess, his attorneys decided not to mention that he and Anderson had been tortured. His defense depended on the lack of evidence against him. Robert Allen was charged only because Tony Anderson implicated him in his tortured confession. This was never introduced at any of Allen's trials. Anderson was only mentioned at Allen's trial as the driver in the initial vehicle stop. The only evidence against Allen was McDermott's testimony, the inconsistent testimony by the witnesses, and the gun recovered from the stolen vehicle that Anderson was driving.

Robert Allen was wrongfully convicted of attempted first-degree murder of Scott Volk, armed robbery, and armed violence for the armed robbery of the Trak Auto Store. He received 55 years for attempted murder, 55 years for armed violence, and 30 years for each of three armed robberies, a total of 125 years. With some of the sentences being served concurrently, Robert Allen's expected discharge date is 2055.

It is necessary to take into account the many injustices individuals suffer, on a daily basis, by the police or by the criminal justice system in general. Robert Allen was illiterate and was convicted based on illegal identifications elicited by the detectives who tortured him. He was only charged because of the coerced confession given by his friend and co-defendant Tony Anderson.

It is not uncommon for poor and illiterate or semi-literate Black men to be railroaded in our criminal justice system. Allen is a survivor of the Burge torture gang, but because he did not confess, the frame-up of this man is being dismissed.

Both Detective McDermott and Detective Maslanka, who interrogated and tortured Robert Allen and Tony Anderson, both testified in the trial of Jon Burge that they engaged in torture, in exchange for immunity from prosecution.

Robert Allen's case demands a hearing on the torture he suffered and the illegal manipulation of false identifications in his frame-up. Pending this hearing, he should be immediately released from custody of the Illinois Department of Corrections.

George Anderson

On August 21, 1991, Claimant George Ellis Anderson, age 29, was arrested and later taken to Area 3 of the Chicago Police Department. George Anderson was questioned by Detectives Michael Kill, Kenneth Boudreau, and John Halloran regarding the homicide that had taken place that same day of Jeremiah Miggins, age 11, who was hit by a stray bullet. Anderson was picked up by the police purely because he was driving down the same street the murder was on. Once at Area 3, Anderson was handcuffed to the wall for over twelve hours with no food or sleep while the detectives continued to ask him if he was ready to tell them about what he did.

Anderson continued to ask why he was being arrested. After Detective Kill informed him that they were going to charge him with the murder of the little boy, Anderson asked if he could have an attorney. The detectives began to beat Anderson repeatedly, including kicking him on the wrists while he was handcuffed to the wall. Anderson was punched in the head, face, and chest. He was threatened with further beatings if he didn't sign a confession. The detectives continued to beat him until Anderson signed the confession handwritten by an Assistant State's Attorney Joseph Brent. Anderson testified that he had signed the confession because he really thought the detectives were trying to hurt him badly and thought they might have killed him if he didn't sign. Detectives Kill, Halloran, and Boudreau stayed in the room and told ASA Brent what to write in the confession. They did not read the statement to Anderson, stating that it didn't matter what it said, because it is what they believed had happened on August 21st.

After Anderson signed the first confession, he was then taken to another room in Area 3 where he was handcuffed with his arms over his head. While in this position Detective James O'Brien and Detective Joseph Stehlik began questioning Anderson about the murder of 14-year-old Kathryn Myles that had occurred on June 9, 1991. Anderson claimed he knew nothing of this incident, and Detective O'Brien held an open telephone book over George Anderson's left side, while Detective Joseph Stehlik struck Anderson with a black rubber hose multiple times. Aggressive interrogation tactics were utilized, including telling Anderson that there was an informant who placed Anderson as the driver involved in the drive-by shooting on June 9th. He was held for over 48 hours in the freezing room with no food or water, asking for a lawyer repeatedly to no avail. As a result, George Anderson agreed to sign a confession, handwritten by Assistant State's Attorney Brian Grossman, confessing to the second homicide case. Anderson had been held in a room with nothing to eat on August 21st, 22nd, and 23rd.

Once Anderson was sent to Cook County Jail, he became sick every few weeks with a high fever, blood while urinating, and pain in his side. He was treated with antibiotics each time, but the cause of the problem was never discovered. After three visits to the hospital, the doctors found that Anderson had a ureteropelvic junction obstruction caused by trauma to his kidney. The doctor at Cook County Hospital stated that this injury was so severe that Anderson could have died due to the kidney releasing toxic waste into the body. Although he had surgery on March 22, 1993, he continues to have kidney problems, and doctors can't tell him exactly what is wrong.

George Anderson recanted his confession and motioned to suppress it from the record. His motion was denied by Judge Joseph Urso based on false testimonies by Detectives Kill, Boudreau, Stehlik, and O'Brien where they denied abusing Anderson. Judge Urso accepted the testimony of the detectives and found that the "evidence shows just to the contrary, that the defendant was not, in fact, physically coerced or forced into giving any sort of statement." After his Motion to Suppress was denied, Anderson was convicted on November 30, 1994, during a bench trial regarding the murder of Miggins, at which his confession was introduced against him. Although Anderson was eligible for the death penalty, the judge imposed a sentence of natural life due to Anderson entering a plea deal on May 24, 1993, for the case involving the murder of Myles. Pursuant to an agreement that he would not be sentenced to death, Anderson received a sentence of 40 years. It took over three years for Anderson to go to trial because of a prosecution stall and due to the fact that Anderson was in and out of the hospital as a result of the injuries accrued from the torture done to him.

Since this initial hearing, new and overwhelming evidence has emerged that the abuse suffered by George Anderson was part of a systematic pattern of torture that occurred at Areas 2 and 3 under Burge's command. Several individual cases show strikingly similar torture tactics with the same detectives.

George Anderson had a court appearance on February 27, 2018, with the presiding Judge William Hooks. This hearing was continued.

George Ellis Anderson's case was reviewed by the Illinois Torture Inquiry and Relief Commission, which decided that, by a preponderance of the evidence, there is sufficient evidence of torture to merit a new hearing. Anderson has been offered a deal by Special Prosecutors Myles, O'Rourke, and Williams to have his case regarding Myles be thrown out, and to serve half the time for his case involving Miggins. George Anderson will not take any deal and is insisting on a new trial. Anderson's case is ongoing and CAARPR will provide updates as they arrive.

Tony Anderson

On April 18, 1990, two police officers followed a car in Chicago, checked the registration and found that it was stolen. The officers stopped the car and questioned Tony Anderson, his wife, and Robert Allen. Anderson and Allen were arrested for auto theft and taken to the police station at 11th and State. There Anderson, age 24, was read his rights and at this time he invoked his right to silence and repeatedly asked to call his family to contact a lawyer. Questioning did not stop. Instead, Anderson was taken to Area 2 where he was questioned by Detectives Michael McDermott and Tony Maslanka. McDermott threatened Anderson by placing a gun to his head and saying he would "blow his damn brains out" if he did not confess. Additionally, Anderson claims that Maslanka physically tortured him by jabbing him in the chest, ribs, and back with his nightstick. Anderson states this happened over 12 times and it was enough to make him cry out in pain. Anderson also states that he made seven requests for permission to make a telephone call and was denied each time.

After enduring repeated threats and beatings, Anderson made an oral statement implicating himself in numerous offenses committed in March and April 1990. He also signed a written confession to the murder of Leonard Cox, which occurred on March 30, 1990. Evidence showed the same gun used to shoot Cox was retrieved from a jacket that was in the car Anderson was driving at the time of his arrest on April 18. Anderson signed a written confession for at least eight other crimes. As a result, Anderson was indicted on over 100 charges in 13 separate cases.

Prior to trial, Anderson's defense attorney, William Heenan, moved to suppress Anderson's confessions because they were the product of police coercion. Based on the verbal and physical torture alleged by Anderson, Heenan stated that his inculpatory statements should not be introduced in trial. Judge Themis Karnezis held a suppression hearing March 19, 1991 through May 1, 1991. Both Detectives McDermott and Maslanka denied any coercion taking place and testified that at no point did Anderson request an attorney. After hearing all of the evidence, Judge Themis denied Anderson's Motion to Suppress, finding that they were given "freely and voluntarily without coercion or threat." Judge Themis stated that the evidence they chose to accept was the testimony of the police officers indicating that Anderson, at no time, was abused or physically threatened.

Following a bench trial, Anderson was found guilty of attempted murder, armed violence, and armed robbery because one of his three confessions (oral) was used against him. He was sentenced to three concurrent terms of 25 years in prison. Anderson then proceeded with a jury trial and was convicted of a separate armed robbery. Anderson was sentenced to 25 years in prison. On August 5, 1991, Anderson was scheduled to have a third trial, but his new lawyer, Thomas

Hoffa, failed to show up in court. Hoffa was found in his apartment two days later, intoxicated and injured, and was sent to the hospital. Judge Karnezis warned Anderson that he had serious reservations regarding the capacity of Hoffa to represent Anderson. Disregarding this warning made by Judge Karnezis, on August 9, 1991, Anderson pled guilty to charges in 11 cases, including one count of first degree murder and ten additional crimes. Anderson pled guilty as part of a negotiated plea where, in exchange for his plea of guilty, he would be sentenced to 50 years for first degree murder, 30 years for attempted first degree murder, 30 years for armed robbery, and five years for attempted escape. The Assistant State's Attorney informed Anderson that there were witnesses who would identify Anderson in each case and they had other incriminating evidence involving Anderson having the murder weapon.

Anderson filed four post-conviction petitions that were all denied without a full hearing. In 1991, Anderson moved to vacate his guilty pleas, claiming that they were coerced, he wasn't aware that he couldn't receive the death penalty, and he was unaware that he could receive consecutive sentences. Judge Karnezis denied the motion saying it was frivolous and without merit. Anderson did not appeal.

In 2000, Anderson alleged that he had been deprived of effective counsel because his lawyer advised him to plead guilty, saying if he proceeded to trial, he would receive the death penalty. Anderson also argued that his counsel was ineffective for failing to file any motions, and for appearing drunk in court on the day of his guilty pleas. Judge James B. Linn dismissed the petition as frivolous. Anderson appealed and the Appellate Court Affirmed the lower court's decision.

Anderson filed his third post-conviction petition in 2004 for his guilty plea to first degree murder. Anderson brought up the coercion and torture that led to his confession and also addressed the newly discovered evidence that coerced confessions were routine at Areas 2 and 3. This included coercion by Detectives McDermott and Maslanka. Judge Linn denied the motion, noting that the voluntariness of Anderson's confession had been adjudicated, all issues had been waived, and the plea had been negotiated. The Appellate Court affirmed, ruling that Anderson had waived the claim that the confession was coerced by failing to raise it in an appeal of any of his post-conviction petitions.

In 2008, Anderson filed a motion covering all of his guilty pleas and claimed actual innocence. Anderson again claimed that his guilty pleas were made as a result of police coercion and ineffective counsel. Judge Linn denied leave to file the petition. The Appellate Court affirmed claiming that this matter had already been decided in previous petitions. The Appellate Court also found that the new evidence of police torture was insufficiently similar to Anderson's claim to justify the petition.

In 2015, Anderson's case went before the Torture Inquiry and Relief Commission. The Torture Commission decided that by a preponderance of the evidence there is sufficient evidence of torture to merit a new hearing. The Commission referred 12 of 13 cases back to the circuit court for further review. The case involving Anderson's attempted escape on April 20, 1990, was left out due to Anderson not confessing to the crime, therefore taking it out of the Commission's referral.

Darryl Christian

On June 24, 1989, 33-year-old Darryl ("DC") Christian arrived at his home to find his stepmother lying dead on the living room floor. He immediately called an ambulance and the Chicago police. Detectives Michael J. Cummings and Lawrence Nitsche were among the responders who questioned Christian, who said he had been at his friend Tiwana Alexander's house until about 4:00 am on June 24th before returning home. After the detectives told Christian that his friend's statement did not support his account, he was arrested and brought to Area 2 of the Chicago Police Department.

Once at Area 2, Christian stated in the TIRC report that he was handcuffed to a wall for several hours and interrogated by Detective Michael Cummings. He was screamed at repeatedly and struck very hard in the face by Detective Cummings and told that the beating would continue if he did not confess to the murder. Fearing further beatings, Christian eventually signed a three-page confession written up by the Assistant State's Attorney David Fischer. Fischer wrote the statement in a separate room by memory of the conversation he and Detective Cummings had had with Christian.

Before the beginning of the trial, Christian filed a motion to suppress his confession, claiming he was beaten into signing it. ASA Fischer, as well as Detectives Cummings and Nitsche, testified against Christian's claims at the suppression hearing. For reasons unknown, Christian's attorney did not call Christian or any other witnesses to the stand to testify at the trial. He also failed to supply any evidence in support of the motion, thus the court denied any claims of coercion or torture.

The trial took place on August 16, 1990, with Judge Ralph Reyna presiding. Also present were Assistant State's Attorney Elizabeth Rivera, Public Defender Kendall Hill, ASA David Fischer, and Detective Michael Cummings. The evidence against Christian was close to none, apart from his confession. There were no eyewitnesses to the stabbing, and the knife used to murder Christian's stepmother was never recovered. The only shred of evidence was a pair of sneakers discovered under the front porch with small traces of blood on the outside of the left heel. An exam concluded the blood to be human, although it was never proven if the blood was that of Christian's stepmother, or if the sneakers belonged to Christian.

There were several inconsistencies in the trial that indicated a coerced confession. The sneakers were never mentioned in Christian's confession. Furthermore, the detectives gathered the clothes Christian was wearing as evidence, and there was no blood found on them, even though the medical examiner concluded that the victim was stabbed 24 times. The detectives claimed Christian had smashed a basement window to make the murder appear to be a break-in, but there were no traces of blood on the window. They also claimed Christian fled in his car to dispose of the knife, but there were no traces of blood or glass in the car.

The confession stated that Christian and his stepmother had had an argument that night about how he should do more housework. Christian's stepmother had then supposedly gone to the kitchen and grabbed a knife, with which Christian stabbed her once before fleeing to drop off the knife. He had then supposedly gone to a friend's house down the street, later returning to the house. As stated above, the main flaw in this story is that medical examiners found his stepmother had been stabbed 24 times, rather than just once, as stated in the confession. Furthermore, Christian appeared to have an excellent relationship with his stepmother, even calling her his mother during questioning. He also paid for her entire funeral—$2,198.00— though he was not well off financially.

Christian was found guilty in 1990 and sentenced to 55 years in prison. He filed a pro se post-conviction petition on February 15, 1994, citing the coerced confession and abuse at Area 2, the lack of evidence, and the inconsistencies between his confession and the evidence presented at the trial. He also stated that the detectives did not read him his Miranda Rights, violating his 5th Amendment rights under the Constitution, nor did they allow him to call a lawyer. Furthermore, Christian claims his counsel, Ms. Williams, showed the jury the pair of gym shoes with blood on them, even though the state did not mention them in the trial or use them as evidence. This made the jury prejudiced against him, denying him a fair trial. The fact that Christian's counsel showed the gym shoes to the jury indicated that Christian did not have his attorney's loyalty. Additionally, he was convicted of murder based solely on his confession, with the prosecution providing no further evidence to corroborate the confession. This petition was denied on procedural grounds without reaching the merits of the argument.

Christian also filed a habeas corpus claim in 1997, stating again that his 5th Amendment rights had been violated due to the coerced confession. This motion was denied in 1998. He made a more detailed claim in his second pro se petition in 2003, citing the 1991 internal investigation into the Chicago Police Department that found systemic abuse at Area 2 under Chief Jon Burge. Christian claimed that the years of abuse at Area 2 gave his claims more merit in court. Christian cited two other cases of police torture, People v. Patterson, and People v. Cannon. Both of these survivors claimed to have been tortured by various police at Area 2 and were granted re-trials as a result. However, Christian's motion was again denied on procedural grounds without an evidentiary hearing and without reaching the merits of the claim.

Christian filed another motion in the Appellate Court on March 4, 2016. In this petition, he cited the Illinois Torture Inquiry and Relief Commission Act, which was established as a result of the Jon Burge torture cases. The Torture Commission found, by a preponderance of the evidence, that there was sufficient evidence of torture, and it referred his case to court for an evidentiary hearing. After reviewing the evidence provided by the TIRC, the Appellate Court denied the motion on the basis that there was no evidence of indisputable error in the Circuit Court's decision. Therefore, Christian's claim was once again denied by the court.

The judge who presided over the original 1990 hearing of Christian, Ralph Reyna, was involved in several trials during the Burge era where there had been clear signs of a coerced confession. Among other survivors was David Bates (1983) who had been beaten repeatedly and tortured into a confession. Reyna also refuses to acknowledge the systematic torture and corruption that defined the Burge era. So, not only the detectives, but also the judge in Christian's trial, was corrupt and had no intention of granting Christian a fair and just trial.

The Torture Commission noted several typical characteristics of a coerced, false confession. The confession itself was very short, considering the murder charge, and the Assistant State's Attorney gave a very limited and unconvincing statement regarding how the confession was provided. It also does not reference important evidence, such as the gym shoes, the murder weapon, and the number of times the victim had been stabbed. The Commission also cited the complete lack of evidence besides the confession, as well as the extremely poor quality of Christian's legal counsel. His counsel did not have Christian testify at his own trial, nor did they provide any witnesses or evidence that would have corroborated Christian's innocence, such as his alibi or evidence that he had paid for his stepmother's funeral. The receipt for the funeral home was only presented 20 years later. The Commission believes a more contemporary hearing would have produced more exculpatory evidence. Finally, Christian's claims of torture have been consistent over the years.

Darryl Christian was paroled in December 2016. His projected parole discharge date is December 2019.

Javan Deloney

On August 8, 1991, 18-year-old Javan Deloney was arrested and questioned regarding two drive-by shootings that had resulted in a triple homicide on Chicago's South Side. Around 10 pm on August 7, 1991, at the intersection of 65th and Peoria and at 516 W 71st there were two related drive-by shootings. In the first shooting, George Cruthard and Marcus Taylor were injured, and Renhardo Bussle was killed. The three men were in front of a building at 6556 S. Peoria where a local gang, the Gangster Disciples, typically sold drugs. Witnesses claimed they saw a red LeBaron and a taxi containing members of a rival gang, the Black Disciples, drive by and begin shooting at them.

A short time later, the same taxi was seen at the scene of another drive-by shooting, which resulted in the injuring of Allen Epton and the killing of John Coleman and Gregory Archibald. Deloney reports he was at his friend Hudson's house at 6:30 p.m. and only left at 6:45 p.m. with another friend, Maurice. They borrowed Hudson's car, a red LeBaron. He reports he returned to the house with the car at 9:30 p.m. Later, while being interrogated, Deloney stated he was at his grandmother's house when the shootings occurred.

There were discrepancies in the evidence and testimonies provided by eyewitnesses. According to eyewitnesses Epton and Brenda Hall, Deloney was present in the taxi that was involved in both shootings on August 7th. Witnesses later changed their accounts in a manner favorable to the prosecution and Cruthard did not identify any shooters until two years later, just before his sentencing in a drug trafficking case. Cruthard recanted this identification in 2013. Additionally, Taylor did not identify any shooters until pressured to do so in 1993. He recanted this identification in 2013. Brenda Hall couldn't accurately describe the shooting and only identified Deloney in a photograph array after the fourth time she was questioned by ASA James McKay in 1993. She recanted this identification in 1998. No fingerprints were found inside the cab connected to both shootings. At this point, there is little to no evidence connecting Deloney to the August 7th shootings.

The detectives who interrogated Deloney, James O'Brien and Daniel McWeeny, are known for having a history of complaints alleging abuse to secure confessions. Deloney's cousin, Maurice, and the other individuals thought to have been involved in the shootings all experienced similar abuse and reported it in 2014 via affidavits. In those affidavits, several people reported hearing Deloney being beaten and screaming in his interrogation room. Additionally, Deloney's mother came to his booking to insist that he be taken to a hospital after his cousin informed her Deloney had been beaten by the arresting officers.

Deloney reports in his testimony that the officers who interrogated him after his arrest verbally abused him, slapped him in the face and repeatedly punched him in the chest and side. Deloney was never told the names of any of these officers and they were in street clothes with no IDs. The officers interrogating him threatened him repeatedly, saying they would keep him there all day if he wouldn't confess. He remained handcuffed to a chair during this ordeal. Deloney was eventually knocked to the ground while the officers repeatedly punched and kicked him in the chest, sides and legs.

Deloney continued to deny any involvement. He asked for a lawyer and to take a lie detector test. Deloney was not read his Miranda rights until approximately 2 a.m. when he was told to sign a confession prepared by the interrogating officers. The confession was written and witnessed by ASA James McKay and Detectives James O'Brien and Daniel McWeeny and then signed by Deloney after hours of interrogation. Deloney was represented by attorneys Larry Dreyfus and Elliot Zinger. Judge Strayhorn tried Deloney's case in 1994, and the jury found Deloney guilty. He was then sentenced to life in prison. In March of 1993 and 1994 Deloney filed motions to suppress his confessions after reporting these statements were coerced by torture. In 1997 Judge Kennelly denied Deloney's petition claiming police brutality.

Deloney's case was taken under review by the Illinois Torture Inquiry Relief Commission on January 18, 2017. They found that by a preponderance of the evidence, there was sufficient evidence of torture of Javan Deloney to merit judicial review.

Javan Deloney is currently in prison at Menard Correctional Center. The Alliance will provide more details as they are available.

Nick Escamilla

On February 10, 1993, I, Nick Escamilla, was illegally kidnapped from my home. Detectives entered my home without an arrest warrant, searched my home without a search warrant, and, without any cause, I was held in custody. My whereabouts were concealed and my constitutional rights were violated. There was absolutely no physical or biological evidence to support the prosecutor's case against me. No actual eyewitnesses existed that could I.D. me, no physical evidence linking me to the crime, no fingerprints, no weapon, no clothing, no car.

Yet, the case moved forward, and I was charged with the first-degree murder of Hector Olague, who was 18 at the time. The murder that I was charged with was at Currie High School. My attorney never investigated this case, never looked at the facts of the case nor did this legal system take the initiative to admit that this case against me was nonexistent. All they decided to do was incarcerate an innocent victim, no matter the lack of evidence, no matter that my constitutional rights were violated, and no matter that the detectives on this case were among the most corrupt detectives on the force. The judge who presided over this case was Dwyer, whose son worked with Jon Burge. I was found guilty and sentenced to 29 years for a crime I did not commit.

The witnesses all gave conflicting clothing descriptions. Some say the shooter had a blue "Duke" jacket, others state a black hoodie. Two witnesses gave vague physical descriptions. I had several witnesses in my favor and a good alibi, but my attorney failed to present or call them at trial. My attorney failed to investigate the background of the state's witnesses, which could have discredited them or shown bias. An admitted gang member with criminal history, who had charges pending, told detectives that he heard through some hearsay that I was involved. This questionable witness was beaten and threatened into identifying me in a photo.

Had my attorney investigated fully, he would have uncovered that my ordeal of being kicked, punched, slapped, and even spit on by officers Halloran, Boudreau, O'Brien, and Ryan was very much a reality because these officers have a history of police abuse. I was threatened with the arrest of my pregnant wife, and the detectives told me they would throw my wife in prison and send my children into D.C.F.S custody if I did not confess to this crime. After 18 hours of torture, threats, no phone call or having an attorney present, I signed a false confession. Detective Boudreau, Halloran, and O'Brien all have extensive histories of police torture and coerced confession out of Area 1. A few years after my confession, F.B.I. investigative reports came out about the Englewood 4, indicating two Cook County State's Attorneys verified a pattern of torture by these detectives that forced detainees into confessing to crimes they did not commit. If I had previously known about this pattern of misconduct by these detectives, I would not have served 14 ½ years behind bars. There have been multiple civil rights lawsuits filed, with some still pending, by over 60 former and current inmates against those same officers. People have been found innocent and exonerated as a result of the uncovering and revealing of the police torture conspiracy. For 25 years, police have framed and terrorized Blacks and Latinx and have built their careers off their backs.

I can list all the victims, but that would take up a lot of space. The list would never stop because, as years go by, more and more evidence comes out that these officers are the real criminals. It is time for our judicial system to stand on the foundation that our forefathers set forth for us. Swing the scales of justice in the favor of all the innocent men and women who have suffered at the hands of these cowards who hide behind their badges. Yet, they swore to protect the lives of the citizens of this great nation in which we live. Justice can only be served by correcting the wrong that has transpired over the many years of our legal system turning a blind eye to the corruptness of the Chicago Police Department.

I have lost so much that I cannot get back, but I know that this city can amend our struggle with a full investigation, pardoning all of us who have been wronged by the actions of these corrupt officers of the law and bringing them to justice.

Darrell Fair

In September 1998, 31-year-old Darrell Fair was arrested at his home for a shooting during an armed robbery outside a nightclub on the south side of Chicago, resulting in the death of Chris Stubblefield. Fair and a co-defendant, Lamont Reeves, were charged with the crimes, and Fair was taken to Area 2 of the Chicago Police Department. There he was interrogated by detectives Przepiora, Porter and McDermott, as well as Assistant State's Attorney (ASA) Adrian Mebane for roughly 30 hours. Upon his arrest, Fair explained to the arresting officers that he had asthma and needed his medication, but he was not allowed to take this medication with him. During the course of the interrogation, Fair was kicked in the leg and threatened with being shot while one of the detectives held his service weapon. He continued to ask for his medication but was denied it. He was also denied food until he agreed to confess to the crime.

The most troubling part of the interrogation is the confession written by ASA Mebane. On the signature line of the first page, Mebane printed Darrell Fair's name. However, Fair never signed it himself. This signature represents a waiver of rights, and without Fair's signature, the written confession is lacking in credibility. According to Mebane, Fair refused to sign the statement without first seeing a lawyer. When asked about why the waiver was not signed by Fair, Mebane had an inconsistent and vague response. He stated that Fair would have signed there and "if he had wished to sign he probably would have signed there indicating that he understood his rights." Based on this statement alone, it appears that Fair was not read his rights properly and gives credibility to Fair's accusations of abuse at Area 2.

Furthermore, none of the corrections made by ASA Mebane, apparently at the request of Fair, were signed by Fair. Once again, Mebane's reasoning for this omission is both confusing and contradictory. In court Mebane initially claimed that Fair only refused to sign the second half of the statement. However, Mebane's testimony indicates Fair would not sign any of the pages because he was not given access to a lawyer. Thus, once again, Mebane loses his credibility in court as well as the credibility of the confession and Fair's involvement in the crime.

Fair's co-defendant, Lamont Reeves, signed a detailed statement, written by ASA Margie Sampson, on August 28, 1998. In it, he describes the events of the crime in a completely different manner than in Fair's supposed confession. In Reeves' version of events, Fair picked him and his friend, Chris, up in his white Camaro and already had the gun under the hood of the car, and the group drove straight to the club where the crime was committed. Reeves stated that Fair then got out of the car and Chris was pointing out the necklace they were attempting to steal from the victim, Stubblefield. Reeves said Fair got in a fight with Stubblefield and that Reeves eventually got the gun out from under the hood and shot him while he was trying to run away.

According to Fair's statement, Reeves put the gun under the hood of his Camaro and the group drove around for about 4-5 hours before heading to the scene of the crime. Fair's statement claimed he stayed in the car while Reeves got out and grabbed his gun from under the hood of the car, approached the person accompanying Stubblefield, snatched his chain and shot him.

While it is not necessarily uncommon for co-defendants to have slightly different accounts of a crime, these two contradict each other in almost every way. Another notable fact to consider is that Reeves signed every page of his confession, while Fair refused to even sign the first page of his confession, which points further towards Fair's credibility.

Fair filed a motion to suppress his confession based on the fact that it was coerced. His claims largely match those he made to the TIRC except for the claim that he was threatened with a gun—which was later taken out of the motion for reasons unknown. This motion was denied. At the jury trial, the verdict rested almost entirely on his confession, as there was no physical evidence other than the car that linked Fair to the crime. He was sentenced to 50 years. After his conviction, he also filed a pro se motion claiming ineffective assistance in getting his original motion through as well as failing to raise the issue of direct appeal, which was also denied based on procedural grounds without an evidentiary hearing.

Fair filed another motion in March 2016 to have his case looked at under the Torture Act, which deals with survivors of abuse at Area 2 during the Jon Burge era. One of the detectives who interrogated Fair, Det. McDermott, worked under Burge. However, the court initially argued that because Fair's abuse occurred after Burge had already been released from duty in 1993, his motion was not under the jurisdiction of the Torture Act. The Appellate Court found that, although the alleged abuse occurred after Burge was released, McDermott had nonetheless worked under Burge, and, thus, the wording of the Torture Act was expanded to include those who had at some point worked under Burge. The court concluded that Fair's claims were within the jurisdiction of the TIRC and that Fair's case was eligible for review by it.

The TIRC concluded, after its investigation, that there was sufficient evidence of abuse for judicial review. These findings were based on the troublesome statement written by ASA Mebane and his lack of a comprehensive explanation, as well as the lack of physical evidence in court, the history of abuse by detectives at Area 2, the contrasting nature of Fair's statement and that of his co-defendant, Reeves, and Fair's consistency in his claims over the years.

Darrell Fair is currently incarcerated at Stateville Correctional Center serving his 50-year sentence.

James Gibson

James Gibson, age 23, was picked up by Area 3 detectives John O'Mara and Phillip Collins on the evening of December 27, 1989, following anonymous tips that Gibson was the shooter at the scene of a double murder resulting in the deaths of Lloyd Benjamin and Hunter Wash. Gibson's brother, Harold, was also implicated in the crime. Both Benjamin and Wash were shot in the head when exiting a garage at 5757 S. May Street on Chicago's south side. Gibson was brought into Area 3 but refused to speak with police. He only continued to say, "I'm not a murderer." He did not confess to either of the murders on that day.

Reports from the days following Gibson's questioning reflect receipt of anonymous tips informing investigators the shooter was James Gibson. Area 2 received a call from an unidentified woman who claimed Gibson was responsible for the two murders and was, at that time, attempting to repair his disabled car with a view toward fleeing the jurisdiction after having attempted to sell the gun used in the crimes.

Gibson was held at Area 3 for questioning for 3 days.

Gibson was re-interviewed on December 29. He stated that on the morning of December 22 he was at a Ms. Davis's home. Upon leaving, Gibson "ran into" his neighbor Eric Johnson and Johnson's brother, who told him the insurance man "just got run over around the corner." According to Gibson, he later found out the victims had been shot, and the word on the street was that brothers "Harp" and "Bodine" were the perpetrators. Gibson also noted that "K.D." Johnson (an alias of Eric Johnson) had suggested robbing the insurance man a month previously, but Gibson had refused to be involved.

Later, on December 29th, detectives took Gibson for a polygraph test and informed him that he "wasn't being truthful in his responses regarding participation and knowledge of the shooting of the victim." Gibson was re-interviewed and told detectives that on December 22 he was approached by Eric Johnson and Bodine who asked him to go with them and rob the insurance man. Gibson said he declined but a few minutes later saw K.D. run into his house and come out dressed in different clothes. Johnson then told Gibson, "We got paid from the insurance man. Keep cool."

Detectives Tony Maslanka, John Paladino, Phillip Collins, and Thomas Ptak were assigned to follow-up on Gibson's statements that night. They first arrested Eric Johnson on an outstanding warrant for an unrelated offense. Detectives then interviewed Johnson and Gibson in succession.

On December 30, 1989, James Gibson gave an inculpatory statement placing him at the scene of the murder. His statement came after three days of detention at Area 3 police station under the command of Jon Burge. He was released without being charged. Upon his release, and prior to his arrest, Gibson filed a complaint with the CPD Office of Professional Standards claiming detectives had beaten him while he was in custody. Gibson alleged that from December 27 to December 30, 1989, at least two unknown white male detectives detained him without charging him for an excessive length of time, physically abused him by slapping, punching, and kicking him, and made physical threats against him. Gibson's sister, Lorraine Brown, who was present when Gibson was released from questioning, observed, "He looked as if they had been in a fight [in the interrogation room], and he told me he had been beaten by police." Ms. Brown then phoned OPS to lodge a complaint and put Gibson on the line. She recalls that Gibson informed the investigator that the officers had beaten him and would not allow him to go to the bathroom so he had to urinate on the floor in the room while being handcuffed to the table.

Gibson maintained his claim of physical abuse to his public defender and doctors after his arrest, and pictures of him depict a swollen, bruised rib cage. A forensic pathologist has advised the Torture Commission that the photos appear to be consistent with Gibson's claim.

On December 31, 1989 Gibson was returned to his residence after Assistant State's Attorney Linda Peters determined additional corroboration was needed before charging him.

Police arrested Gibson later in the evening of December 31 after police received approval following a series of signed statements from defendants Johnson and Webb and a series of polygraph tests taken by all three defendants.

Johnson later moved to suppress his statement on the basis that it was coerced by physical abuse. Johnson stated that he signed a statement he did not write or review because he "was tired of getting beat" and was told that if he signed he would be able to go home.

Gibson's public defender, Paul Stralka, sought and received a court order permitting his investigator to photograph Gibson. Investigator Martorana took pictures of the left and right sides of Gibson's chest and his buttocks and noted that "injuries are all of swollen areas." The pictures depict swollen, tender regions around Gibson's ribs. Medical records from Cermak Health Services dated January 3, 1990, state that Gibson sought medical assistance because he had been "hit by police" and that "he was beaten up." Records also reflect that he had bruises on his ribs.

On March 13, 1990, Investigator Jose Ortiz interviewed Gibson by phone from jail. Gibson identified Detectives Collis and O'Mara as the aggressors and stated that they had punched him in the ribs and neck area approximately 30 to 40 times, kicked him in the groin area twice, and slapped him about 7 times, and further threatened to "beat the shit out of him."

Both detectives submitted affidavits denying any physical abuse had been observed or had occurred during the questioning from December 27, 1989 to December 31, 1989. All affidavits were addressed to their commander, Jon Burge.

Gibson and Stralka, Gibson's public defender, were present at the suppression hearing on February 14, 1991.

Stralka and Gibson created motions to 1) quash his December 31, 1989 arrest based on lack of probable cause, 2) suppress statements of Johnson and other witnesses, and 3) suppress statements from Gibson after his 1989 arrest.

All of Gibson's motions were denied by Judge Richard Neville due to lack of independent corroboration via medical records, as well as testimony from offending detectives saying they saw no signs of aggression or violence during the interrogations of December of 1989. The Court also found that Johnson was not credible and refused to suppress his statement.

Gibson's bench trial began on Oct. 7, 1991. Carla Smith (Johnson's sister), Detective Moser (took confession statement from Gibson), and Fernando Webb (originally identified by Gibson as the shooter) testified at the trial against Gibson.

During this trial, the judge stated:

"I think that based on what I have just heard Mr. Gibson put himself in this statement at the scene of the incident and also indicates that he knew the incident was going to take place...the State can argue inferentially that he was doing something there to assist, and that, I think, is sufficient."

Based on evidence presented, the judge found Gibson guilty. The Court concluded both Johnson's sister and Webb were credible.

Carla Smith testified on cross-examination that she had been asked to come to the police station on December 29, 1989 and was told that upon giving her statement her brother, Eric Johnson would be able to leave. Carla Smith stated that she had not read the statement she then signed.

The court concluded that both Johnson's sister and Webb were credible. Based primarily on his inculpatory statement, Gibson was convicted of first-degree murder and sentenced to life in prison.

Gibson immediately filed an Attorney Registration and Disciplinary Commission (ARDC) complaint against his attorney, Stralka, on the basis that he did not permit Gibson to testify and did not present Gibson's alibi defense. The court later denied a motion for judgement of acquittal based on the lack of sufficiently credible evidence to support a conviction.

In 1993, Gibson appealed his conviction on the following grounds: 1) the State's failure to prove his guilt beyond a reasonable doubt, and 2) ineffective assistance of counsel, based upon his lawyer's failure to call alibi witnesses.

The Appellate Court found the evidence sufficient to support a conviction. It also found Stralka's failure to call alibi witnesses did not constitute ineffective assistance of counsel.

Gibson, thereafter, filed successive post-conviction petitions alleging ineffective assistance of counsel. These petitions were denied by the Circuit Court. The Appellate Court also found Stralka's failure to present alibi witness did not materially alter the outcome of Gibson's trial. The Illinois Supreme Court denied a Writ of Certiorari.

In 1999, Gibson filed another petition for post-conviction relief, alleging that the prosecution knowingly induced Carla Smith to offer unfavorable perjured testimony. His petition was denied by the Circuit Court and on appeal.

In 2003, Gibson sought a Writ of Habeas Corpus from the Northern District of Illinois. He again alleged ineffective assistance of counsel based on Stralka's failure to present alibi witnesses and alibi defense, failure to permit Gibson to testify at trial, failure to interview and investigate other witnesses, and failure to provide Gibson a legal copy of the police reports. His petitions for reconsideration and leave to appeal were denied.

In 2005, Gibson filled another petition for post-conviction relief regarding Eric Johnson's statement being included in the trial. This petition was denied.

The Illinois Torture Inquiry and Relief Commission reviewed Gibson's case in 2015 and found that, by a preponderance of the evidence, there was sufficient credible evidence of torture to merit judicial review.

James Gibson's case was heard by the Illinois Supreme Court, and on March 22, 2018, they reversed and remanded his case back to the lower court for further proceedings. The Supreme Court found that when the two accused officers, John Byrne and John Paladino, invoked their fifth-amendment rights against self-incrimination, an adverse inference should be found because there was no credible reason for refusing to do so. The Supreme Court decision stated, "a law-enforcement officer's refusal to answer these allegations under oath is not to be taken lightly." This decision by the Illinois Supreme Court is very important and is likely to have a great impact on several other torture cases where officers invoked their fifth-amendment right.

Awaiting a new trial, James Gibson is currently incarcerated at Stateville Correctional Center, serving his life sentence.

Anthony Jakes

On September 16th, 1991, Anthony Jakes ("AJ"), 15 years old, was arrested and questioned regarding the deadly shooting of Raphael Garcia after a botched armed robbery. His interrogators at Area 3 Homicide were Detectives Michael Kill and Kenneth Boudreau, members of the notorious "Midnight Crew" of torturer Jon Burge. Jakes was interrogated for 16 hours during which he was severely kicked, slapped, punched, and beaten, sustaining injuries to his back, stomach, knee, elbow, and ribs. Kill also threatened to throw Jakes out the window and even stated that he would use his connections with the Latin Kings gang to "jump on" Jakes's family if he refused to confess. In order to end the beatings and fearing for his family, Jakes signed a four-page confession, written by Kill. Jakes was eventually indicted for murder and attempted armed robbery. His forced confession was the only evidence used to convict Jakes.

The case was assigned to Judge Thomas D. Durkin. At the initial court proceeding on September 15, 1991, photos of his injuries were presented. They depicted the heavy bruising throughout his body sustained from the hours of beating. Jakes's defense filed a Motion to Suppress his forced confession, and the photographic evidence was introduced. However, Kill and Boudreau insisted the injuries were the result of a gang fight. A doctor from the Audy Home (Juvenile Temporary Detention Center) testified that when he talked to Jakes he never mentioned being beaten by the police, nor did the injuries look recent. The motion was denied because the judge found Kill and Boudreau more believable than Jakes, who was found guilty and sentenced to 40 years in prison for two crimes he did not commit. After losing the direct appeal in 1995, Jakes filed a petition for post-conviction relief which bounced around the court until finally being dismissed by Judge Michael P. Toomin. The case was reassigned to Judge Nicholas Ford in 2008, who dismissed it in September 2011, also denying a motion to grant Jakes access to records of cases of abuse and misconduct at the hands of Kill and Boudreau.

In 1990 the Office of Professional Standards of the Chicago Police Department concluded, after an internal investigation, that there had been widespread systematic abuse in Area 2 under Police Chief Jon Burge. Jakes's trial took place after this discovery, but before the report was publicly released in 1992 . Upon further investigation, it was discovered that Kill was accused of torturing 20 other survivors. Furthermore, roughly 90% of the suspects in Kill's 1,500 murder confessions filed Motions to Suppress, based on unnecessary use of physical force.

Jakes was eventually released in 2013 after serving 22 years of his 40-year sentence. In December 2013, the Appellate Court decided that Judge Ford had abused his power when he dismissed Anthony's petition. They sent his case back down to the lower court to have an evidentiary hearing on Kill's and Boudreau's misconduct. In January 2015 the Post-Conviction Petition, along with the Torture Commission referral, were brought before Circuit Court Judge William Hooks. Kill testified, defending his investigation techniques, as well as admitting to using the N-word.

In August 2015, at the Leighton Criminal Court Building in front of Judge William Hooks, Jakes was able to testify on his abuse at the hands of Kill and Boudreau. During the trial, Jakes's attorney, Russell Ainsworth of the Chicago Exoneration Project, showed Kill a photograph of the lockup at Area 3 where Jakes was being held. It depicted hands clutching prison bars with the phrase, "another happy ending," written on the bottom. Kill claimed to have no knowledge of the photo nor of whose hands were depicted in it. According to the Chicago Tribune, Kill avoided answering questions directly and seemed confused about the various reports and transcripts throughout the trial. Kill's general demeanor throughout the questioning was laced with snide comments, frequent scowling and visible frustration at the questions being asked.

Although Jakes was eventually released, he does not have a driver's license and was unable to even graduate high school. His adolescence and young adulthood were robbed from him by a forced confession. It has been difficult for Anthony Jakes to return to everyday life after being unjustly behind bars for so long. Unable to receive a proper education, he now works as a janitor and claims his "dreams are shot," according to the Chicago Tribune.

Jerome Johnson

On the evening of August 21, 1991, 19-year-old Jerome Johnson was arrested and transported to Area 3 of the Chicago Police Department to be questioned about the shooting of Jeremiah Miggins, age 11, and Kathryn Myles, age 14. Johnson was held in an interrogation room for over 24 hours with nothing to eat or drink. He was repeatedly slapped in the face and kicked in the wrists where his handcuffs were. Johnson was ultimately indicted on the two homicides based on the tortured confessions he gave.

According to Assistant State's Attorney Joseph Brent, the homicide of Kathryn Myles occurred on June 9, 1991. ASA Brent alleged that Johnson and other individuals devised a plan to shoot up the area of 66th St. and Wolcott Avenue in retaliation for a previous altercation. In doing so, he said, Johnson fatally shot an innocent bystander, Kathryn Myles. The second shooting was a gang-related dispute that led to the fatal shooting of Jeremiah Miggins, another innocent bystander, on August 21, 1991.

Jerome Johnson was interrogated by Detectives Michael Kill and John Halloran on August 21, 1991. ASA Brent also came in and questioned Johnson about the murder of Miggins. When Johnson refused to sign the written statement, two officers came into the room and beginning slapping him in the face and kicking him in the wrists. Johnson continued refusing to confess. So the officers left him in the dark, hot interrogation room for several hours with no food, water, or access to a bathroom.

Detectives Kenneth Boudreau and Michael Kill returned with ASA Brent on the morning of August 22, 1991, at which point Jerome Johnson signed a handwritten statement, written by ASA Brent, confessing to the murder of Jeremiah Miggins. Johnson was then taken back to the interrogation room where Detectives James O'Brien and Joseph Stehlik began questioning him regarding the shooting of Kathryn Myles. Questioning continued throughout the entirety of August 22 and didn't end until midnight on August 23 when Johnson signed a handwritten statement, written by Assistant State's Attorney Brian Grossman, confessing to the murder of Kathryn Myles.

Jerome Johnson was held in an interrogation room from August 21 through August 23 with nothing to eat or drink and without bathroom accessibility. Although many detectives testified that they offered use of a bathroom to Johnson, none testified that they ever took Johnson to a bathroom or gave him any food during this period.

Jerome Johnson filed a Motion to Suppress both confessions on March 4, 1992. Johnson filed this motion on the grounds that the statements were obtained as a result of physical, psychological, and mental coercion and were therefore involuntary, in violation of the 5th and 14th Amendments of the U.S. Constitution. Johnson's Motion to Suppress hearing was held on June 25, 1993. During this hearing Johnson testified to the treatment that he experienced in the interrogation room prior to making his confession. He stated that he had signed the first statement after a long night in a hot, dark room under the promise made by ASA Brent that after he signed he would be free to go. Detectives Halloran, Kill, O'Brien, and Stehlik, along with State's Attorneys Brent and Grossman, also testified during this hearing. At the conclusion of the hearing, the judge determined that there had been no physical, psychological, or mental coercion and, thus, denied the motion to suppress the statements in both criminal cases against Johnson.

Jerome Johnson pled guilty to the murder of Kathryn Myles after the prosecution used Johnson's confession as factual basis for the plea. For the case regarding the murder of Jeremiah Miggins, Johnson went to trial. Johnson's attorney, Deborah Gubin, attempted to prohibit the introduction of the Myles homicide conviction in the event that Johnson took the stand. The State opposed this motion, stating they intended to introduce the conviction as a way to discredit Johnson if he took the stand. The State won, and Gubin did not call Johnson to the stand during trial, as the prosecution would have introduced the statement Johnson had made, and she would not have had the ability to attack and discredit the statement.

Johnson was found guilty of first-degree murder and two counts of aggravated battery with a firearm. Johnson was eligible for the death penalty but was sentenced to natural life in prison.

On July 25, 2011, Jerome Johnson filed a Petition to Withdraw Guilty Plea and Vacate Sentence which was denied as frivolous.

Johnson filed a complaint with the Torture Commission on September 11, 2011, stating that his conviction was wrongful because it was based on the confessions obtained through torture. The Torture Commission began interviews with Johnson on April 6, 2015. On March 28, 2018, the Torture Commission concluded that there was sufficient and credible evidence of torture to refer Johnson's case back for further review because Johnson's torture allegations have been largely consistent throughout the decades and due to the numerous allegations made by other claimants against Detectives Halloran, Boudreau, O'Brien, Stehlik, and Kill, who were named in Johnson's claim.

Jerome Johnson is currently incarcerated at Stateville Correctional Center serving his life sentence.

Note: This case is very closely related to another included in this booklet, George Anderson. These two individuals were convicted of the same murders of Kathryn Myles and Jeremiah Miggins. Johnson and Anderson were tried separately so as to not confuse jurors as to how two individuals could be convicted of killing the same people.

Scott Mitchell

On January 20th, 1996, 24-year-old Scott Mitchell was taken to Area 1 at 51st and Wentworth, where he was interrogated and tortured for approximately 33 hours by Chicago police officers Joseph Danzl, Glen Turner, and others, who previously worked under the supervision of torturer Jon Burge. He was questioned regarding the murder of Michael Mickey and wounding of Marvin Harris that had occurred during the course of an armed robbery. Mitchell, who according to his mother had already suffered two prior severe head injuries, was hit repeatedly with a book during the course of his interrogation, which he tried to ward off with his hand. Mitchell was also punched in his stomach and chest hard enough to make him cry. Danzl, using a trick reminiscent of Jon Burge's tool kit, threatened to arrest Mitchell's mother on unrelated charges which would have meant DCFS taking custody of Mitchell's siblings. Mitchell summarily made a court-reported confession.

When Mitchell was brought to Cook County Jail, he complained of pain in his chest and right thumb. Before his trial his court-appointed public defenders, Gary Coyne and Rita Fry, helped him file to suppress his confession. Even with testimony from the Cook County Jail Medical Intake Worker, the police denied mistreatment, and Judge Henry Simmons denied the motion.

Mitchell was convicted of first degree murder and attempted first degree murder after he entered a negotiated plea of guilty in exchange for consecutive sentences of 30 and 15 years imprisonment for the murder of Michael Mickey and wounding of Marvin Harris. Upon sentencing, he also received three years of Mandatory Supervised Release.

On October 13, 2011, Mitchell, serving as his own attorney, filed a Post-Conviction Petition that was the basis of his appeal. He asserted his three-year Mandatory Supervised Release term extends his imprisonment beyond the 45-year sentence to which he agreed when he pled guilty and that he was not advised of that possibility. He further argued that his due process rights were violated because he did not receive the benefit of his plea agreement. Mitchell asked that the MSR period be removed from his sentence or that his 45-year sentence be reduced to allow the MSR term to be served within the 45-year term.

On December 9, 2011, the Circuit Court and Judge James Obbish summarily dismissed Mitchell's post-conviction petition.

On July 25, 2013, the Illinois Torture Inquiry and Relief Commission stated that there was a preponderance of evidence that Mitchell had been tortured, given the length of interrogation, the background and allegations of torture by Danzl,

Mitchell's psychiatric history, mental faculties, diagnosis of paranoid schizophrenia, and his complaint of injuries during medical intake at the Cook County Jail. In May of 2016, his appeal in the Appellate Court under Judges Matthew E. Coghlan and Maura Slattery-Boyle, was reversed and remanded back to the circuit for further decision.

Scott Mitchell was paroled in June 2017, and he is projected to be discharged in 2020.

Kevin Murray

Kevin Murray, age 24, and co-defendant, Tyrone Washington, were convicted of a double murder on September 11, 1990. During interrogations, from January 18 through January 20, 1988, detectives beat Murray. Murray claims that as a direct result of this sustained abuse, he gave a coerced confession to murder. He signed a written confession that led to his conviction for murder and was sentenced to natural life in confinement. Murray and Washington were both convicted of the gang-related double murder of Brain Fowler and DeJuan Buck. This case was heard before Judge Thomas Maloney, who has a history of proven corruption that calls into question any case that is brought before him.

The murders of Fowler and Buck occurred in November of 1987. Co-defendant Tyrone Washington alleges that he was the shooter while Murray drove the getaway car. After detectives contacted Murray's mother to get in contact with Murray, he voluntarily agreed to meet with the detectives to answer questions. However, before he could go to the station he was handcuffed and brought into custody by Detectives Kriston Kato and John Summerville.

Murray was escorted by police to the station while accompanied by his aunt because he was a minor at the time. After his aunt left, Murray was placed in a room alone with Detective Kato who began to punch and kick him repeatedly. The detectives told Murray that he would leave and come back and, if Murray did not answer the questions, the beatings would continue. When Detective Kato returned 15 to 20 minutes later, he asked the same questions, and when Murray gave the same answers the detective kicked and hit Murray again repeatedly.

At this time, Murray asked the detectives to bring his girlfriend in to corroborate his story and answers. When his girlfriend arrived, he attempted to tell her about the abuse, at which point she was taken away immediately. The detectives returned and told Murray his girlfriend had told them the truth, and he was lying. They began to beat him again, punching him in the head and stomach. The detectives then brought in Washington, who named Murray as an accomplice. The officers proceeded to ask Washington questions in front of Murray. Washington's answers were different from Murray's. Murray said the co-defendant was lying and his beating continued. At this point, around 2 a.m., Murray asked for his aunt or to call his mom so she could get him a lawyer. The detectives told him no.

Murray was left alone in the interrogation room without food, or water, or the option to use the bathroom until 4 p.m. the next day. When the detectives returned, they told Murray he had to take a polygraph test. He was moved to another location to take the polygraph. Later, when he returned to the police station, Detective Kato proceeded to kick and slap Murray. Detective Summerville arrived in the room and barricaded the door with a chair, and also began to kick, slap, and punch Murray repeatedly. Murray submitted and agreed to do anything the detectives wanted.

Murray asked Summerville again for a lawyer, at which point Summerville mocked him and then started punching Murray again. Murray once again said he would do anything Summerville wanted. Summerville stopped, and Kato came back in and said "See, I told you, if you did what we want you to, you could have been home by now." Kato then started rehearsing the statement with Murray. Shortly after, Murray's statement was taken by ASA Lavin. Murray was told that if he signed the confession he could go home. There was a lack of any physical evidence against Murray, which may have provided a motive to induce a confession.

Other than the vague testimony of Washington, there was no evidence at the time of the arrest, or afterwards, that Murray was guilty of a crime. Murray testified that everything in his court-reported confession was false except his name. A jury convicted Murray on September 11, 1990 under Judge Thomas Maloney, who sentenced him to life in prison. In 1993, Judge Thomas J. Maloney was convicted for a series of judicially corrupt acts. He was charged with "fixing" three murder trials between May 1981 and June 1985.

In 2013, Murray filed his first Post-Conviction Petition. Murray said he had never filed any prior Post-Conviction Petitions because he didn't know the legal system, didn't trust jailhouse lawyers, and couldn't get anyone to represent him.

The Illinois Torture and Relief Inquiry Commission concluded, in March of 2017, there was sufficient evidence of torture to merit judicial review for Kevin Murray's case.

In this case, the chief detectives, the presiding judge, and the attorney who briefly represented Murray (and testified on his behalf) were all found guilty of misdemeanor or felony crimes, casting doubt on their credibility. In addition, the lack of any notes by police officers and the lack of a felony review memo by the State's Attorney who took the confession are troubling. Combine those irregularities with the lengthy abuse allegation histories of Detectives Summerville and Kato and the various authorities' convictions, and there is sufficient evidence meriting judicial review. Murray is still incarcerated at Stateville Correctional Center, serving a sentence of natural life while awaiting a new trial and justice for the cruel treatment he received.

David Randle

The case of David Randle involves a possible coerced confession to the homicide of Sophie Lorek, an elderly woman in Randle's neighborhood. Randle knew Sophie through working odd jobs for her, the last one being on December 14, 1990, when he fixed a toilet for her. On December 18, 1990, Sophie Lorek was found in her kitchen with a butcher knife at her feet and a pool of blood around her. A medical examiner later revealed that she had three stab wounds to the chest and one slash wound to the neck. She died due to these wounds, though a time of death was unable to be ascertained. There was broken glass on her window sill, though the detective on the case, Detective James Boylan, did not believe it was possible for someone to have entered through the window. Therefore, it is not certain how a person came in to commit the murder.

The following is the story that was introduced through the confession of David Randle. There were no witnesses, and the only evidence is the coerced confession that Randle signed. During the incident, it was claimed, Randle was fixing Sophie's toilet while she was engaged in a heated argument on the phone. When Randle emerged from the bathroom, Sophie ripped the phone out of the wall and was waving a wooden-handled kitchen knife at him. It was after this knife was waved at Randle that he took it from her, shoved her, and proceeded to stab her. The chain of events alleged in the confession was bizarre. There also appears to have been no motive or reason for Sophie to pull the receiver out of the wall, attack Randle with the knife, and have him take it from her.

It was also alleged that David Randle had taken Sophie's snub-nose Colt revolver, which was the basis on which Detective James Boylan went to Randle's home and put him under arrest. Supposedly, Detective Michael Tillman's son told him he had seen Randle with this snub-nose revolver and about $1,000. After hearing this information, Detective Boylan went to Randle's home and arrested him on January 4, 1991. The court found that the police had probable cause to do so, given the evidence of the revolver. On a subsequent court date, Randle was allowed to reopen the hearing on the motion. In this hearing, Detective Tillman testified that his only son was not in Chicago during December 1990 or January 1991. Tillman also denied he had told the police that his son had any knowledge of the murder. Though he said this, Detective Boylan and Beverly Draper, a police dispatcher's aide, both testified that they did have the conversation about the revolver with Tillman. Boylan and Draper's statements overruled the new testimony given by Tillman, and it did not change the court's previous ruling of probable cause. Though this is the case, it is important to note that this revolver has never been found.

Detective Boylan and his colleague, Detective Timothy McDermott, were the ones who began the interrogation of David Randle. Randle insisted he did not have any knowledge of what had happened to Sophie Lorek. He also said he had gone to a motel that night with his brother, Frank, and two girls, and that he had paid for this hotel room in cash. His brother had been taken to the police station alongside Randle, though nothing was documented regarding what occurred after this.

Later, Detectives George Basile and George Wilkins spoke with David Randle at Area 2 while Detective Boylan and his colleague were out questioning Randle's brother. Area 2 is of significance, as it was later found to be a place that had many reports of torture occurring, with an investigation discovering that out of 142 cases half of them had involved abuse or torture. When Wilkins left the room and Randle was alone with Basile, Randle made his admission that he was at Sophie Lorek's house on the night of the murder. It is believed that Detective Basile was the main perpetrator of the coercion of Randle into a confession. Randle later signed a statement, written by Assistant State's Attorney Matthews, that he had been treated fairly. Though he did this, he later stated that he had not read the statement before signing it. His conviction at trial was also almost solely based on his confession. There were no eyewitnesses or physical evidence placing Randle at the crime scene.

David Randle was also denied medication. He was supposed to take Dilantin, three times daily, for seizures. When Detective Basile heard of this, he dropped the bag of his Dilantin on the floor and stepped on it. After denying Randle his medications, he then proceeded to grab his testicles and kept squeezing them until he finally confessed that he had stabbed Sophie Lorek. When he went to the hospital to finally get his medications, he told the doctors of his hurting testicles. Randle has consistently alleged that, during the course of questioning at Area 2, Basile had squeezed his testicles in order to get a confession.

A clinical psychologist, Dr. Robert Wilson, examined Randle and said that he had a very low IQ and suffered from perceptual abnormalities, attention deficit problems, and a lifelong learning disability, all which could have affected his ability to understand his Miranda Rights or what exactly was going on during his trial. Randle's later representatives have since argued that he had ineffective assistance of counsel in these matters, as "his trial counsel fell below the objective standard of reasonableness in two aspects: (1) the failure to call Dr. Robert Wilson or any other mental health professional at the hearing on the defendant's motion to suppress, or at trial, and (2) the failure to call the doctor from Cook County jail as a witness at the suppression hearing."

Judge Egan presided over this case on December 29, 1995. David Randle's attorneys were Charles H.R. Peters and Daniel S. Brennan of Schiff Hardin & Waite, in Chicago. ASA Matthews, Detective Boylan and Detective Basile were all major players in this case. Since the motion to suppress, the systemic abuse in Area 2 over the last 10 years was subsequently discovered, and Jon Burge was suspended from the Police Board of Chicago after he was found guilty of abusing another person in Area 2. There was a report released that concluded that abuse was an ongoing practice in Area 2. On direct appeal of his conviction, Randle argued that the trial court had made a mistake in thinking that his confession had been voluntary and not coerced. The Appellate Court deemed ASA Matthews to be more credible than Randle in these matters. At the initial jury trial, Randle was convicted of first-degree murder, armed robbery, and felony murder. He was sentenced to serve 100 years in the Illinois Department of Corrections. His rehearing was denied March 5, 1996. In 2003, Randle tried raising his coercion claim in a Successive Post-Conviction Petition, but it was dismissed on procedural grounds without the merits of the case actually being reviewed. Even after this, Randle repeated his claim of coercion to the Special State's Attorney, but the case was closed because of lack of corroborating evidence.

The Torture Commission reviewed this case in 2012 and found that there was cause for the review, stating, "By a preponderance of evidence, there is sufficient evidence of torture to conclude the Claim is credible and merits judicial review for appropriate relief."

David Randle is currently on parole and is projected to be discharged on December 15th, 2018.

Tortured for 27 years!

Gerald Reed

On October 3, 1990, 27-year-old Gerald Reed was arrested and questioned regarding the murder two days earlier of Willie Williams and Pamela Powers. He was questioned by Detectives Michael Kill and Victor Breska at Area 3 Homicide, members of the notorious "Midnight Crew" of torturer Jon Burge. On October 4, 1990, Reed was questioned by Kill and Breska. They beat him and kicked him repeatedly and broke a metal rod that was in his right thigh along with the surgical screws that held it in place, causing him excruciating pain. The rod had been surgically placed years before to repair his thigh-bone, which had been shattered by a gunshot.

It was clear to Reed that the beatings would continue until he agreed to confess, and he did. Prior to trial, Reed filed a motion to suppress his confession stating that he had been physically abused. He repudiated the confession at his trial and has proclaimed his innocence ever since. There was no other material evidence against Reed at his trial. Gerald Reed was convicted of both murders and sentenced to life in prison without possibility of parole.

But that did not stop the torture. For 27 years, Reed has repeatedly requested medical intervention to fix the horrible and excruciatingly painful damage done by his torturers. He has been unable to walk. Finally, last year, he was taken from Stateville Correctional Center to Dreyer Medical Center in Aurora, where orthopedic surgeon Steven I. Rabin performed the first step required to repair the terrible damage to his thigh bone and ease his suffering. Dr. Rabin made it clear that a second follow-up surgery was necessary to improve his condition and end his pain, along with physical therapy.

Gerald Reed was returned to the hospital at Stateville in January where he waited for the second surgery. Dr. Rabin, however, had a heart attack and was unable to complete the task. Gerald Reed has been in the hospital at Stateville ever since, for over ten months. He has had minimal physical therapy and is still suffering from serious pain in his leg.

The Illinois Torture Inquiry and Relief Commission held, in a decision rendered on June 18, 2012 and further amended on March 19, 2014, that there was a "preponderance of evidence" that Reed had been tortured and forced to confess. Yet, more than 5 years later Gerald Reed remains in prison and in terrible pain as a result of being tortured by Chicago Police.

Gerald Reed's case is currently being heard by Judge Thomas Gainer. Since the Torture Commission has sent his case back for review, Reed has had an ongoing torture review case for more than 6 years. Gerald Reed's mother, Armanda Shackleford, hopes to have him home in early 2019.

Clayborn Smith

On October 20th, 1992, Clayborn Smith's grandfather, Miller Tims, and great aunt, Ruby Bivens, were murdered in their home, and his great uncle, Herbert Tims, was assaulted before their house was set on fire while they were still inside. Clayborn Smith, age 22, was later arrested and brought to Area 1 by Chicago police for questioning regarding his involvement.

Once Clayborn Smith arrived at Area 1, he was interrogated for 39 hours by Detectives John Halloran, Kenneth Boudreau, and James O'Brien. During that time he was threatened, beaten, and jerked around by his braids with enough force that they became detached from his head. He was presented with misinformation and false evidence regarding his case during this time and ended up signing a court-reported confession under duress.

Smith later filed a Motion to Suppress this confession and testified to support this motion. He testified that he had been tortured into confessing. He also testified he had been with his girlfriend and friend during the time of the murder. His alibi was later corroborated by his girlfriend, Karen Tate, and his friend, Rodney Sisson. This Motion to Suppress his coerced confession was denied. Smith was convicted of two counts of murder, one count of assault, and one count of arson, at trial, and sentenced to natural life without parole.

Clayborn Smith has consistently stated that his confession was coerced. His story matches many accounts (Ivan Smith, James Gibson, Javan Deloney) from other cases under investigation that accuse the Chicago Police Department of abusing and torturing people, while detained, in order to obtain a false confession.

There are several pieces of evidence that were either not presented at trial or have emerged since this hearing. Since Clayborn's initial trial, all three of the detectives who interrogated him have been investigated for abuse and coercion of witnesses. Detective Halloran has since been accused of 39 cases of abuse and coercion. Many of those survivors were individuals who were beaten until falsely confessing to crimes they did not commit. Detective Boudreau has since been accused of 37 cases of abuse and coercion. Many of his victims reported hair pulling similar to Smith's account. Detective O'Brien has since been accused of 35 cases of abuse and coercion, likewise including complaints of survivors beaten until they confessed to a crime they did not commit. Finally, all three of these detectives, when questioned about abusing detainees, have consistently pled the Fifth Amendment while under oath in court.

Smith's initial confession had significant inconsistencies with the evidence found at the crime scene. For example, Smith never mentions anything past "poking" his grandfather with a fork, though there were 17 lacerations visible on the body, and 7 of those stab wounds were an inch or deeper. Additionally, he went into detail regarding the injuries caused to his great aunt but failed to mention strangling her with a telephone cord as the crime scene report showed. Finally, Smith's confession stated that he had started one fire in the kitchen, but the report showed there had been at least two fires started in the house with a trail of gasoline in the house.

Without his tortured confession, there is no evidence tying Clayborn Smith to the crime.

The Illinois Torture and Inquiry Relief Commission reviewed this case and found that, by a preponderance of the evidence, there is sufficient evidence of torture.

At this time, Smith's case has been referred back to court for review and is currently being reviewed due to the Commission's findings. He is currently represented by Joel Brodsky. CAARPR will provide more information as it becomes known.

Ivan Smith

Ivan Smith, age 18, was arrested in November 1991 in Ripley, Tennessee, for two gang-related shootings in Chicago that left three dead and three others injured. On the evening of August 7, 1991, Smith, a member of the Black Disciples street gang, drove by a building in the territory of the Gangster Disciples, a rival gang, and yelled a Black Disciples slogan while throwing up a gang sign. One of the bodyguards shot at Smith's car from inside the building, and Smith reportedly drove away, saying he would be back.

Around 10 or 11 that night, George Cruthird and Jerome Taylor were selling drugs in front of the same building with Taylor's cousin, 13-year-old Rhenardo Bussle. Cruthird stated that three cars drove up to the building. The occupants of a taxi, between the other two cars, rolled down the taxi's windows and began shooting at them before driving away. Rhenardo Bussle would later die of his gunshot wounds. A few minutes later, the same taxi was reportedly used in a second drive-by shooting, killing John Coleman and Gregory Archibald. There were several witnesses who identified the taxi but there were mixed reports on who had been driving.

Two detectives investigating the shootings, James O'Brian and Joseph Stehlik, found a taxi, matching the descriptions given by witnesses, abandoned in a nearby vacant lot. No fingerprints were found inside. The following day O'Brian found a gray Chevette with bullet holes in it that had a temporary license plate identifying Ivan Smith as the owner. The car then disappeared until it was found a year and a half later. The Chevette had not been examined by police when O'Brian initially discovered it. Although Cruthird and Taylor would eventually give statements implicating Smith, they did not mention him in their initial discussions with police shortly after the shootings.

Shortly after the crimes, Ivan Smith went to Tennessee, where his mother lived. He was arrested in November 1991 and taken to Lauderdale County Jail in Tennessee, where he was held for two to three hours. While there, he was handcuffed and choked by arresting officers for being a "city slicker" and accused of coming to Tennessee to cause trouble. He was told Chicago police were coming, and then he was transferred to Tipton County Jail, where he claims jail guards did not mistreat him.

A day later, he was met by Detectives O'Brian and Stehlik, Assistant State's Attorneys Michael Smith and Charles Burns, and court reporter Janet Lupa. When the detectives asked him about the murders, Ivan Smith asked for his mother and a lawyer. Both requests were denied. O'Brian, Stehlik and Michael Smith then took him to the cafeteria. Ivan Smith was told that his fingerprints had been found in the taxi, an outright lie, and that his co-defendant, Terry Brooks, had not yet made a statement, so they needed Smith to testify against him.

When Smith refused, O'Brian slapped his face and asked if he was going to cooperate. When Smith again asked for his mother and a lawyer, O'Brian struck him in the back of his head. Smith, who was handcuffed by the ankle to the desk, stood up in response. Stehlik called Tipton officers and ordered them to handcuff Smith's hands behind his back. O'Brian asked Smith another question and then punched him in the chest when he did not respond. O'Brian continued to punch him in the chest and force his shoulders onto a bench. Stehlik then laid a phonebook on Smith's chest and used a stick to repeatedly strike him on the chest, making it hard for Smith to breathe. When Smith remained silent upon further questioning, the beatings continued. The detectives said they would bring Smith back to Chicago and "do it the right way" after which Smith agreed to cooperate and gave a 21-page statement to the court reporter. Smith also claimed, in following appeals and post-conviction petitions, Michael Smith had coached him on what to say in the statement. The next day, Illinois authorities drove him by Elvis Presley's home and ordered him to make gang signs while they took photos.

Once Ivan Smith was back in Chicago, he asked a guard for medical attention, saying his chest hurt due to the beatings. The guard did not believe him and did not let him obtain medical attention. Smith was eventually taken to Cook County jail at 26th and California to await trial, where he claims no abuse occurred.

Before his trial, on February 10, 1993, Ivan Smith filed a Motion to Suppress his confession as evidence on the grounds that it was coerced. At the suppression hearing, Smith and his attorney, Rita A. Fry, claimed that his confession had been obtained as a result of psychological and mental coercion and, thereby, forced out of Smith. The statement cited the false report by the detectives that fingerprints had been found in the taxi and the threats that the beatings would continue if he did not confess. Furthermore, Smith claimed that he had not been read his Miranda Rights nor had he been given the opportunity to contact a lawyer or his mother, which he had repeatedly requested. In conclusion, Smith asked that any oral or written confession that came from the interrogation be suppressed in the trial. However, the suppression was denied by Judge Earl Strayhorn after the prosecutor made a rebuttal argument against it.

On May 12, 1994, a jury found Smith guilty of three counts of murder and two counts of attempted murder. Smith, Brooks and Javan Deloney were found guilty, while Milshap and Maurice Deloney were acquitted. Smith filed several appeals, all of which were denied. In 1996, he filed a motion stating that ASA Burns should have been cross-examined. In 1997, Smith filed a Post-Conviction Motion which the judge found frivolous and denied. Appeals of that decision were again denied in 2000 and 2001. In 2002, Smith filed a Habeas Corpus Petition in federal court. However, the judge ruled the coercion issue procedurally defaulted.

There are many irregularities noticeable in the interrogation and retrieval of Ivan Smith. The sheer size of the group, ordered by the Chief of the Cook County State's Attorney's Office's Criminal Bureau, to fetch Smith from Tennessee had been unusually large, even for a murder suspect. Even the detectives acknowledged in their testimonies that it had seemed unnecessary to bring along two detectives, two ASA's, and a court reporter. Furthermore, both Burns and Stehlik denied that they were there to obtain a confession from Smith, even though it would have been completely normal to admit this. Burns only admitted this fact after long deliberation with a defense attorney. Their unwillingness to admit this only decreased their credibility.

Detectives O'Brian and Stehlik also contradicted each other at the suppression hearing when asked if they had told Smith everything they knew about the crime during their interrogation. O'Brian stated they had not, while Stehlik claimed they had. Stehlik denied that anyone had requested a room for the interrogation. However, O'Brian told the TIRC that officials at Tipton served prisoners their food in their cells for the specific purpose of using the cafeteria for the interrogation. It is unlikely that the jail authorities would go to such great lengths if a specific request had not been made. This controversy further discredited Stehlik.

Finally, there had been several present during the interrogation who claimed they had to get a typewriter for the court reporter from another county. However, Tipton Sheriff Buddy Lewis claimed they had plenty of typewriters in the building and had never needed to fetch one from anywhere else. Ivan Smith claimed he had been interrogated for roughly two hours, as opposed to the authorities's claim of 30-60 minutes. This was covered up by the fictitious lack of a typewriter at the jail.

There are many other factors that support Smith's claim. One is the abuse of Smith's co-defendants, specifically Curtis Milsap. A Cook County Jail guard, Roland Allen, testified that he would not accept Milsap into his wing at the jail because of bruising and a noticeable limp. Milsap alleged he had been slapped in the face and kicked in the testicles during his interrogation. Milsap said no one believed him until he started peeing blood. Co-defendant Javan Deloney also cited abuse by interrogators, although he was not able to identify them at the trial. He stated that he saw guards strike and knock Maurice Deloney to the ground at the station.

The majority of supposed evidence against Ivan Smith is based on the testimonies of George Cruthird and Jerome Taylor, who were members of Smith's rival gang, the Gangster Disciples. There were major problems with these testimonies. First, Cruthird and Taylor had conflicting accounts of what exactly had happened that night. Cruthird said he saw three cars with the taxi in the middle, while Taylor remembered only seeing two cars. Taylor also testified that he was not able to see the driver's face. Another fact that casts doubt on their credibility is that George Cruthird had been facing drug charges at the time of his statement. It is likely that Cruthird had been given special treatment in return for his statement, given that he received the minimum sentence for his crime. Taylor, whose cousin was killed in the shooting, said he was under immense pressure from his aunt, who was Rhenardo Brussle's mother, to give a statement implicating Smith. Both key testimonies were possibly false.

Much of the evidence that was presented against Smith, besides the testimony of his gang rivals, relied on eyewitness accounts of the crime. Many of these accounts don't specifically mention Smith, only different variations of a man driving the taxi. One witness stated seeing only one man in a white hat emerge from the taxi. The majority of the witnesses, even those wounded during the shootings, recanted their identification. Some of the detectives involved in the initial case have pleaded the fifth amendment in other cases. It is insufficient evidence that no one had been able to initially identify Smith. More problematically, these key eyewitnesses recanted their previous claims.

One of the most compelling factors supporting Smith's claims is that Detective O'Brian had a total of 36 complaints filed against him, one of which, by George Anderson, was also against Detective Stehlik. Of those cases, two were deemed valid, 21 were deemed invalid by the court, eight were unfounded, and O'Brian was exonerated in four of the cases. Although O'Brian was essentially cleared in most of the cases. The sheer number of complaints speaks against him. Of 18 complaints on record with the Chicago Police Department, 12 cited physical force used to obtain or attempt to obtain a confession. O'Brian had a clear pattern of abuse during his interrogations.

Of these complaints, the two most notable are those by George Anderson and Robert Wilson. Anderson filed a complaint against both O'Brian and Stehlik, claiming the two detectives forced his confession by placing a phonebook on his chest and beating him with a pipe or hose, strikingly similar to the account of Ivan Smith. Robert Wilson's complaint against O'Brian was deemed "not sustained." Robert Wilson, who had been charged with slashing a woman's face at a bus stop, had been slapped multiple times in the face by O'Brian, and told to confess. Wilson had confessed after 30 hours in custody. Five weeks after his arrest, five similar attacks on women subsequently occurred, but the judge at the trial refused to admit these attacks as evidence in court. After the victim recanted her statement, claiming she had initially told O'Brian and other detectives that the attacker looked much older than Wilson. However, the detectives had pressured her for an identification. Wilson was later exonerated after he was retried and received $3.6 million in settlement money in a 2012 lawsuit against O'Brian, the city and Cook County. Again, Wilson's allegations of being slapped in the face by O'Brian are very similar to those of Ivan Smith, proving these torture methods were used often by O'Brian.

On January 20, 2016, the Illinois Torture and Relief Commission concluded that, by a preponderance of the evidence, there was sufficient evidence to conclude Ivan Smith was tortured. This was based on the contradicting statements and claims of abuse of the co-defendants, O'Brian's patterns of abuse, Stehlik's and O'Brian's reluctance in admitting they were in Tennessee to obtain a confession, though acknowledging this was the reason for traveling with such a large group. In addition, there was the strong likelihood that a co-defendant of Smith was also tortured, and that neither the detectives nor the Assistant State's Attorneys present took any notes during the initial interrogation.

Ivan Smith is currently incarcerated at Hill Correctional Center serving his life sentence.

Robert Smith

On September 19, 1987, 39-year-old Robert Smith was arrested and questioned for approximately 18 hours regarding the double homicide of Edith Yeager and Willie Bell. Smith claimed innocence. Edith and Willie, Robert's mother-in-law and grandmother-in-law, were found in Yeager's home with their throats cut and the house on fire. Smith was initially arrested for obstructing justice, but was later charged with both murders after confessing while in custody, a confession he says was coerced. Assistant State's Attorney Ray Brogan and Detective William Higgins were present at the time of the confession. Detectives William Pedersen, Steven Brownfield, and Daniel McWeeny, the latter of the two having numerous allegations of abuse, were assigned to the case in the Area 2 Violent Crimes Unit. The Illinois Torture Inquiry and Relief Commission has determined that Smith was beaten, kicked, choked, and threatened with further violence if he did not confess to the murder.

In February 1989, there was a Motion to Suppress hearing. Smith wanted to quash his confession, claiming it was coerced. He told of being taken into a questioning room at Area 2, handcuffed to a wall, and kicked in the chest by one detective. After that detective left, two more came in, one calling him a "cold-blooded killer," and said they had found something with his blood on it. This caused Smith to scream and call for help from his wife and uncle. One officer responded by shoving a handkerchief down his throat and choking him until the second detective told him to let go. These officers then proceeded to tell Smith that he had committed the perfect crime, which angered Smith. To calm him down the detectives then offered him cigarettes and coffee. Ten to fifteen minutes later, two more officers came into the room and accused him of the murders. Smith began cursing after this, and one of the officers responded by slapping him on the head.

After further questioning, Smith began asking if he could see a doctor, as he had been in the hospital earlier that day. The officers refused his request and told him he could not until they were finished. They proceeded to slap Smith again before leaving to check his alibi. Two more detectives came in after they left, one calling him a "piece of shit husband." The officers continued to question him, but Smith responded that he did not know who committed the murder and he had been playing pool in a tournament all night. After Detectives Pederson and Brownfield left, another two came in who were described as being "harder" than the prior two. One told Smith he "didn't like "n*ggers" and he was going to "splatter [his] Black butt all against this wall." Then the officers ordered Smith to pull down his pants, and he obeyed. He was not wearing underwear due to having a rash on his penis. The officers then showed him some bloody underwear and asked if they were his, to which he responded, "Yes." Though they were his, Smith never told them that he had dropped the underwear while washing his clothes after committing the murders.

Two more officers came into the interview room. One told Smith he was a man of God, and the other told him he had a party to get to and he "didn't have time to mess with no n*gger all night." Smith testified that at that time he was very tired and scared, and his sides hurt as if he had some broken ribs. He also said he was coming down from a high. All of these concerns were voiced to the detectives. After this, another two detectives came into the room. One made Smith take off his shoes and saw blood on the side of his foot and took a blood sample to the lab. The other one told Smith to just make it easy on himself and tell them what he did. Lieutenant Cline told Smith he could go to the hospital if he gave a statement before a state's attorney. Smith testified that he had told Assistant State's Attorney Raymond Brogan the detectives had beaten him, to which Brogan replied, "they ain't doing nothing like this to you." He brought in another detective. By this time, his nerves were shot, he had not been given his medication, had been up since 6 a.m., and had not eaten since arriving at Area 2. Hungry, exhausted, beaten, and physically deteriorated, Robert Smith gave in to their demands, finally agreeing to "cooperate."

The case went to trial In August 1990. The judge found Smith guilty of first-degree murder of both Yeager and Alexander, and he was sentenced to natural life in prison. Following the trial, Smith filed for a direct appeal. In this appeal, he argued that "he was not proven guilty beyond a reasonable doubt, his Motion To Suppress was improperly denied, he was unlawfully arrested without probable cause, the physical evidence and statements obtained after his arrest were the fruits of an illegal arrest, his confession resulted from physical and mental coercion, he did not voluntarily waive his Miranda rights, and the trial counsel was ineffective for failing to present evidence of his severe head injury, subsequent complications, and medication." The Appellate Court still affirmed his conviction and sentence.

Smith then filed his first Post-Conviction Petition on April 24, 1996. In this petition, he asserted two claims: The trial counsel improperly allowed him to testify at trial, and the trial and appellate counsel were ineffective for failing to assert that his right to a fitness hearing was violated because he was on psychotropic medication at the time of the trial. The circuit court dismissed this Post-Conviction Petition at the first stage after deciding that the defendant had not been on any medications and that his attorney had clearly discussed whether he should testify at trial and decided that he should not. The Appellate Court affirmed the trial court's dismissal of his Post-Conviction Petition on appeal.

Robert Smith also filed a Habeas Corpus Petition in federal court in 1998. In this habeas petition, Smith alleged: "ineffective assistance of counsel for failure to present evidence of his medical conditions," "appellate counsel was ineffective for failure to argue that trial counsel should have requested a fitness hearing," "the police lacked probable cause to arrest him and that his confession was coerced," and "there was insufficient evidence to convict." The district court denied the petition.

In 1999, Smith filed a petition for mandamus relief requesting records and reports from his psychological and psychiatric evaluations in 1987 and 1988. The court denied this petition as well.

In October 2006, Smith filed a section 2-1401 petition for relief from judgment, arguing that there was new evidence of systemic police abuse by officers and detectives in Area 2 during the time he was in custody, citing the Report of Special State's Attorneys Edward Egan and Robert Boyle on systemic police abuse in Chicago (2006 report). Upon reviewing the section 2-1401 petition, the trial court made the observation that, given the newly alleged discovered evidence, the court would have granted Smith's motion to suppress his confession to the murder charges. It had been a due process violation. The court stated that, as it was a constitutional claim, it would be assigned to the docket as a Post-Conviction Petition and referred to the Public Defender's Office. The case was then transferred to a new judge.

During the transition, the Attorney General's Office took over the case from the State's Attorney's office. The Attorney General then filed a motion to dismiss the 2-1401 petition. A public defender never appeared on behalf of Smith for the motion, and the Attorney General's Office served a copy of the motion to Smith, personally. Smith asked for extra time to respond, but he ended up not responding, which led the court to dismiss the case. The Attorney General was responsible for sending Smith a copy of the order dismissing his petition. However, he reported he had not received notice of this dismissal until May 2011, and there is nothing recorded to counter this.

In August 2011, Smith filed another Post-Conviction Petition, which claimed: "his confession was involuntary and given as a result of physical coercion," and "the state violated Brady V. Maryland (1963) by failing to disclose the evidence of torture at Area 2." His claim that Area 2 detectives tortured him is also based on his testimony that was given at the suppression hearing. Additionally, at this hearing the Report of the Special State's Attorneys Edward Egan and Robert Boyle, that was released in 2006, was brought to the attention of the court, alongside his ability to specifically link detectives's names to their actions of abuse during his interrogation. Smith claims that: Officer Martin Rios kicked him in the chest; Detective McWeeny punched him in the sides with handcuffs wrapped around his fist; Detective McGovern choked him and stuffed a handkerchief in his mouth until he lost consciousness; Detectives William Higgins and William Pederson struck him in the face; and Detectives Robert Rice and Steven Brownfield threatened to "slam [his] n*gg*r *ss all over this room." Lastly, Lieutenant Philip Cline refused to let Smith see the doctor until he confessed.

On September 8, 2011, the trial court dismissed Smith's Post-Conviction Petition. This was due to the trial court interpreting the petition as making a Brady, which means that was claiming he was actually innocent. Since Smith had not raised the abuse at Area 2 prior to publication of the 2006 report, and said report not having changed the outcome of his initial trial, they waived this petition. There was no discussion in the trial court's order of Smith having been denied leave to file his successive Post-Conviction Petition of his due process claim that his confession had been a result of coercion.

Smith filed an appeal in a timely manner. The final decision was filed under Supreme Court Rule 23. Presiding Justice Howse delivered the judgment of the court. Justices Lavin and Epstein agreed in the judgment. That decision states that they affirm the trial court's denial of leave to file a successive Post-Conviction Petition with respect to Smith's Brady claim, as that claim was waived. However, they reversed the trial court's denial of leave with respect to Smith's coerced confession claim and decided that he had established the requisite cause and prejudice necessary to be granted leave to file a successive Post-Conviction Petition due to that claim. Thus, prior proceedings were affirmed, in part, but also reversed, in part, and remanded for further proceedings.

Accusations of torture were corroborated during the Torture Commission's review through the subpoenaed medical records of Robert Smith, which confirm that he was, indeed, treated for a skull fracture. Although a motion to dismiss was filed and ruled against, Smith's medical records were not introduced as evidence in the motion's hearing. The judge, then, did not have access to evidence that would have exonerated Smith and refused to dismiss the testimony based on issues of credibility. Since only Smith had testified to the mistreatment, the judge assumed it must not have happened.

The Commission asserted, in a decision on July 25, 2013, that the confession "exhibits many of the standard characteristics of a coerced, false confession case," the prosecution's case "without the confession was almost nil," and "the confession was a quick, 'easy' solution to the case." Robert Smith remains, almost five years after it was determined that he was tortured, incarcerated based on a coerced and unsubstantiated confession which he had refused to sign.

Robert Smith has been incarcerated for almost 30 years after a trial that relied heavily on an unsubstantiated, flawed, and minimal confession that was obtained through torture. Smith should have his case reheard immediately, given the context of his confession.

Sean Tyler

Sean Tyler has been targeted by the Chicago Police Department since he witnessed the fatal shooting of Alfredo Hernandez on September 25, 1991, outside Tyler's childhood home. Tyler later testified that 13-year-old Marcus Wiggins (Marcus Wiggins's case is discussed further elsewhere in this booklet) was wrongfully accused of this murder. Tyler was initially hesitant to testify due to his fear of retaliation from the police but eventually did since the Chicago Police Department was attempting to frame Wiggins for a crime he did not commit and brutally tortured him in order to obtain a coerced confession. Tyler's testimony proved Wiggins's innocence and shined a light on the Chicago Police Department's history of violent abuse during interrogation. Wiggins and his family went on to successfully sue the Chicago Police Department and settle after the court findings proved there was evidence to support Wiggins's claim. While Tyler's testimony was necessary to exonerate Wiggins, it created a volatile relationship between Tyler and the Chicago Police Department.

Although Tyler was promised protection and anonymity if he testified, that clearly was not the case. The judge overseeing Wiggins's trial placed a protective order on Tyler from the detectives involved in Wiggins's case. Detectives Kenneth Boudreau, James O'Brien and Jack Halloran all served under the historically problematic Commander Burge. They were made aware of this protective action but were also the detectives who framed, interrogated, and tortured Tyler years later.

Ten-year-old Rodney Collins was fatally shot on March 29, 1994, around 5 p.m. at Winchester and 51st. These previously mentioned detectives looked to frame Wiggins again for this crime, but Wiggins was able to prove he was out of the state, in Wisconsin, during the time of the murder. These detectives needed a new suspect to blame and turned to Sean Tyler. There was no physical evidence or motive to connect Tyler to this crime. The only evidence against Tyler was a coerced confession, after a 2-day period of abuse, and witness statements, that have since been recanted on the grounds they were forced by police.

Detectives picked up neighborhood kids Michael Taylor, Antoine Ward, and Kenneth McGraw based on very little information and violently interrogated them. Ward's and McGraw's accounts were almost identical. They reported being held for two days while being beaten and encouraged to confess to a crime they did not commit. When this proved fruitless, these detectives picked up Michael Taylor. He was interrogated by the same detectives and was forced to sign a pre-written confession that tied him to the Collins murder. When Taylor initially refused to sign the confession, he was violently beaten and handcuffed to a coat rack. He was denied access to an attorney and was never read his rights. When he was given food, the detective interrogating him dumped his cigarette ashtray on the food to keep Taylor from eating.

After their unsuccessful attempts to frame these three young men, they arrested Tyler's brother, Reginald Henderson. Henderson denied involvement and asked for his parents, a request which was denied. He was grabbed by the throat by detectives and threatened with "50 years in jail." He was then left shackled to a wall for 7 hours. When detectives returned, they handcuffed him to a chair and repeatedly smacked him on the ears from behind. They also smashed his head into a desk. During the 48 hours Henderson was in custody, he was not given food or water, allowed to use the restroom, or read his rights. Finally, Henderson agreed to confess that he and his brother were involved in Collins's murder.

Sean Tyler presented himself at Area 1 when he heard that police were looking to speak with him regarding the Collins murder. He denied involvement and provided his alibi. Tyler had three alibi witnesses, Donald Jones, George Mosley and Steven Alexander, who confirmed spending the evening playing video games with Tyler. He was beaten when he continued to refuse to confess to the Collins murder. The detectives left the room and returned with a signed confession from Henderson implicating both him and Tyler. Tyler agreed to sign it after he began vomiting blood and had to be taken to the hospital for emergency medical attention.

Sean Tyler's present petition includes medical records showing he was vomiting blood when admitted from the police station. The doctors who treated Tyler diagnosed him with hematemesis, which is consistent with the chest trauma that was inflicted on him while he was interrogated. There is no alternative explanation for this diagnosis other than violent and repeated beating to his chest. At trial, the state reported that this diagnosis must have been linked to his previous history of asthma. There is no evidence that Tyler's episode of vomiting blood was related to asthma or that he ever had a previous history of this symptom before interacting with police. Two separate witnesses saw Tyler shortly after his interaction with police and confirmed his face was swollen and bruised.

In terms of actual evidence, there is almost none. As stated previously, there is no physical evidence that Tyler committed this crime and no motive. Tyler has an alibi. He was arrested and interrogated by the same detectives from whom Tyler was protected by a court-ordered protective act. Aside from the coerced confession, the only thing connecting Tyler to this murder was one witness, Andrea Murray, who had been at home during the shooting and reported seeing two boys fleeing the scene past her kitchen window after the shots. She had called 911 after she heard the gunshots.

Years after the trial, Murray confirmed, in an affidavit, that she had been paid "relocation money" and been "bought" in order to testify against Tyler. She had been new to the neighborhood and detectives had threatened her. Murray had been paid to move by having her moving fees, first month's rent, and security deposit covered. Murray stated that this payment was no small factor in her decision to testify.

Murray stated later that she couldn't see well enough through her window to identify anyone. Detectives had shown her Tyler's and Taylor's photos and told her she had to pick them out of a lineup. A new trial should be granted on the grounds of witness discrepancy, alone. She was not a disinterested witness, as previously reported by the State, and has since recanted her testimony. Murray only identified Tyler after being shown a photograph of him by detectives. Murray has stated in a Post-Conviction Petition that what she did was wrong and would like to see that justice is done.

Over half a dozen eyewitnesses to the shooting were interviewed. Not one was able to identify Tyler. These witnesses were Charles Breckenridge, Maurice Judon, James Barber, Phillip Smith, Thomas Larson, David Larson, and Marquan Grey. Charles Breckenridge stated that police had encouraged him to identify Tyler as the shooter. He reported he saw the shooters and was positive they were not Tyler. He testified under oath stating this. At trial, no eyewitnesses of the shooting identified Tyler, and, even after coercion, Murray only identified Tyler as a boy who was running past her apartment. Additionally, Tyler's counsel made no attempt to introduce the evidence regarding the Hernandez murder as an explanation and clear connection as to why these detectives were targeting Tyler. His counsel also didn't attempt to show the history of violent behavior among these detectives. Finally, Tyler's counsel didn't attempt to present evidence that showed there was another person with the same nickname as Tyler (Droopy) in their neighborhood who later pled guilty to the murder of Rodney Collins.

Throughout the trial, all of the aforementioned detectives pled the fifth regarding bribing Murray, encouraging eye witnesses to identify Tyler, beating alleged suspects while denying them basic human and civil rights, and using unethical methods of investigating the murder of Rodney Collins. Even with no evidence and circumstantial witness testimonies, Tyler was sentenced to 58 years in prison in September 1995. In October 1998, Tyler filed a Post-Conviction Petition (PCP) in order to address several issues with his case ranging from actual innocence to errors in counsel and violations of multiple constitutional amendments. This PCP asked for: an outright reversal of his conviction; the vacating of his conviction followed by a new trial; and/or a hearing at which proof might be offered concerning the allegations contained in his petition.

Most recently, in February 1999, Tyler appealed to have the court suppress his coerced confession and also asked the court to take into account some things such as his age, rehabilitative capacity, lack of criminal background, lack of violent background and a disproportionate sentencing compared to other cases. At this point, the court lowered his sentence to 50 years.

Vincent Wade

Vincent Wade was arrested around 6 p.m. on August 13, 1984, for the home invasion and murder of Tyrone Tolliver on August 9. According to Tolliver's girlfriend, Melba Martin, who witnessed the crime, Wade and an accomplice, Michael Lynch, entered the home and asked about a "stash." They believed Tolliver was a cocaine dealer. Martin testified she was set free and, upon leaving, heard a gunshot. Police later found Tolliver shot and stabbed several times on the bathroom floor and bound at the hands and feet. Lynch was found in California a couple of years after the crime and was brought to Chicago for trial.

Wade was brought to Area 2 of the Chicago Police Department where he was tortured until 12:45 a.m. on August 15. According to Wade, who was just 15 at the time, he was interrogated by Detectives Michael Hoke, Frank Glynn, George Karl, and John Paladino. On the ride to Area 2, Wade had been continuously beaten by one of the detectives. Once at Area 2, Wade was not given access to a lawyer and was again beaten. He was struck multiple times in the eye and stomach, kneed in the groin, repeatedly struck with a "baton-like stick" on his chest after a large phonebook was placed over it, and struck in the nose with a flashlight. As a result of this abuse, Wade signed a written confession to the crimes.

On August 16, 1984, Wade gave a written statement to the Office of Professional Standards (OPS) providing a detailed account of his abuse at Area 2, and, while he did not know the names of the detectives at the time, he gave a description of them. The OPS concluded in 1992, after an internal investigation, that there had been sufficient evidence of systematic abuse at Area 2 for over 10 years.

Three photos, taken two days after Wade's arrest, were introduced as evidence of the abuse. These photos showed a mark under one of his eyes as well as a cut on Wade's nose. Detective Hoke testified that the mark under Wade's eye was due to his having fallen during his arrest. Hoke was unable to determine where the cut on his nose came from but later claimed it had also resulted from a "scuffle during the course of the arrest." The Torture Commission determined this claim to be contrary to the first claim that the mark under Wade's eye was the only injury. The TIRC found that this corroborated Wade's claims of physical abuse. Although Wade filed a motion to suppress his confession, the motion was denied. He was subsequently found guilty, almost entirely based on his confession, and sentenced to life in prison for the murder.

There are several allegations of torture made by other survivors against three of the detectives who interrogated Wade. There are 24 other cases of torture against John Paladino, and both Frank Glynn and Michael Hoke have each been accused of physical abuse in four cases. All three detectives have claimed their Fifth Amendment rights in these cases. Though not an admission of guilt, it does not help the credibility of the detectives.

Among the 24 other accusations made against detective Paladino, several of them noted abuse similar to what Wade had experienced, such as being beaten with a flashlight, being hit in the chest, and being threatened. Furthermore, several of Paladino's victims were also quite young—one of them as young as 13. Michael Hoke had often participated in interrogations alongside Jon Burge, such as in the case of George Powell, who was repeatedly shocked, "bagged," and beaten by Hoke and Burge. Wade's claims are strikingly similar to those of other survivors of abuse at the hands of these detectives, notably when Detective Hoke placed a phone book over Wade's chest and beat him with a baton-like stick. This is similar to two other TIRC cases: those of George Anderson and Ivan Smith.

Wade has made several appeals to the courts to have his confession suppressed and his sentence changed, but these have been unsuccessful. On June 28, 1989, Wade filed an appeal stating he had not, in fact, delivered the wounds that killed Tolliver, and he should not have received life imprisonment for the crime. Judge David Cerda of the Appellate Court denied this motion, affirming the court's original judgement, and finding Wade's arguments to be insufficient to yield review. Another motion was filed on March 12, 2014, when he appealed to judge Paul Biebel under the Post-Conviction Hearing Act. The motion was denied because not all requirements were met to present a valid claim under the Act.

The Torture Commission concluded there was substantial evidence of torture. This was based on several factors, including Wade's consistency, over the years, in his claims of abuse and the striking similarity between Wade's statement and others who had suffered similar abuse at the hands of the detectives at Area 2. Furthermore, Wade's statement to the OPS was consistent with their findings of abuse at Area 2. The dozens of other accusations against the detectives who had interrogated Wade largely resembled those of Wade himself. Finally, the fact that the detectives who had interrogated Wade all invoked their Fifth Amendment rights spoke to their lack of credibility.

Shawn Whirl

On April 18, 1990, cabdriver Billy G. Williams was shot in the head and killed. His death was blamed on Shawn Whirl, age 20, who was arrested, charged, and incarcerated for over twenty years, until 2015 when he was exonerated. As tragic as the death of Billy Williams is, no justice is served when the wrong person is incarcerated.

Whirl's story of wrongful conviction and incarceration is tragic and is a tale of police abuse and torture. On April 18, 1990, Shawn Whirl (then 20 years old) was out purchasing feminine products for his fiancée. He then went to head back to his mother's house where he lived. He arrived at the el station at 87th and the Dan Ryan where he was approached by three known gang members. They asked him about the hat and jacket he was wearing and, then, knocked him down onto the train platform. Whirl's left leg got scraped on the edge of the platform when he fell. Whirl quickly got up, pushed the other gang member over, and ran toward the front of the approaching el train. He quickly got on the train to evade these men but was unsuccessful in doing so. Whirl arrived at 95th and the Dan Ryan, got off the train, and saw that the three gang members were still following him. He ran over to a gas station and hid behind a parked cab.

At this point, the prosecution wove a very persuasive story, saying that Whirl had gotten into the cab, driven by Billy Williams, and asked Williams to take him to several places before eventually telling him to go to 820 E. 103rd St., the parking lot of Gately Stadium. Here, the prosecution claimed, Whirl had told Williams that this was a stick-up and that he was going to rob him because he had seen a bag of change in his cab. According to the prosecution, Whirl shot Williams in the head, took the bag of change, and ran away, dropping the gun in some unknown location.

Whirl was arrested by the Chicago Police and was interrogated by Detectives William Marley and James Pienta. Detective Pienta had, by then, a twenty-year history of abuse and torture under his supervisor, Commander Jon Burge. When Whirl refused to confess to the murder of Billy Williams, Pienta handcuffed Whirl to a wall in the interrogation room and began instructing Whirl what to say to the detectives. Whirl was kept in the interrogation room for several hours and fell asleep. Pienta returned and woke Whirl by stepping on his ankle, calling him the n-word, and beating him. Pienta attempted to coach him into a confession. When Whirl still refused, Pienta took a key from his keychain, and dug it into the already existing leg wound that Whirl had (from his injury on the el platform). He continued to torture Whirl in this way until Whirl correctly repeated a scripted confession. To muffle Whirl's screams while Pienta carved his key into Whirl's leg, Pienta took a potato chip bag (from a snack they had given Whirl) and stuffed it into Whirl's mouth.

Under these conditions, and after about twenty times of having his leg carved into, Whirl eventually provided a confession to the Assistant State's Attorney, Richard A. Stevens. Detective Pienta was present while Whirl gave his confession and even signed the statement after Whirl finished giving it. This confession was given in an interrogation room at the Area 2 Headquarters at 727 E. 111th St.

Prior to trial, his attorney, Mark Lyon, motioned to suppress Whirl's confession, but this was denied by the Judge, William Cousins Jr. The prosecution gave their version of the story of the murder of Billy Williams. The defense attested to the lack of evidence against Whirl: no murder weapon was ever found, and no forensic evidence was found, save for one fingerprint found on the front passenger door of Williams's cab. The defense surmised this print was from when Whirl had hidden behind the cab while running from the three gang members. Had he actually been inside the cab and sitting behind the driver, as the prosecution alleged, his fingerprints would have been on the rear driver's side door and the inside of the cab—which they were not.

Ultimately, Whirl pled guilty to the crime, in fear of capital punishment if it went to trial. On October 7, 1991, he was sentenced to sixty years in prison for first-degree murder and attempted armed robbery.

In 2008, Whirl filed a Post-Conviction Petition seeking to vacate his plea, citing that he had not been informed at the time of his plea that he would face three years of mandatory supervised release. This petition was dismissed as "frivolous."

Whirl filed another post-conviction petition in 2011, citing his actual innocence. He attached records and affidavits from other defendants alleging a pattern of physical abuse of suspects by Detective Pienta. Included in this petition was a signed statement by a witness who had seen a gang member chase Whirl back in 1990 and who saw this gang member get into Billy Williams's cab. According to this witness, it was common knowledge in the community that the gang member who had chased Whirl was the murderer of Billy Williams. In April 2011, the trial judge refused to allow Whirl to file this petition, because Whirl had not consistently claimed police torture in previous petitions.

Yet, by this time, plenty of allegations of police torture and abuse had been made against Chicago Police Lt. Jon Burge and the detectives under his command. Therefore, Whirl appealed the decision dismissing his petition. In February 2012, attorneys from the Exoneration Project at the University of Chicago Law School and the People's Law Office filed another Post-Conviction Petition on Whirl's behalf. This petition was based on findings from the Torture Commission that concluded Whirl's case did include sufficient evidence of police torture and merited judicial review for appropriate relief.

In 2013, Whirl amended his Post-Conviction Petition and cited evidence of the pattern and practice of detectives under Jon Burge's command coercing false confessions through torture and physical abuse. In November of 2013, the petition was dismissed. The judge agreed that there was enough evidence of torture by other detectives but that Whirl was not credible and had not established that he had been tortured.

Finally, in August of 2015, the Illinois Appellate Court reversed this dismissal. The Appellate Court vacated Whirl's conviction and ordered that he be granted a new hearing on a motion to suppress his confession. The Court also noted that Detective Pienta repeatedly invoked his 5th amendment right against self-incrimination when questioned about the interrogation. The appellate court stated: "The new evidence presented at the post-conviction hearing, when weighed against the prosecution's original evidence was conclusive enough that the outcome of the suppression hearing likely would have been different if Pienta had been subject to impeachment based on evidence of abusive tactics he employed in the interrogation of other suspects." They further noted: "Indeed, it is impossible to conceive of how the prosecution could prevail at a new suppression hearing with the officer alleged to have coerced a suspect's confession invoking his privilege against self-incrimination."

Thus, on October 13, 2015, the prosecution dismissed the charges and Shawn Whirl was released. Whirl filed a federal civil rights lawsuit that was settled by the City of Chicago for $4 million in January 2017.

Marcus Wiggins

In 1991, Marcus Wiggins was only 13 years old when he was arrested without probable cause following a gang-related shooting. The victim was 16-year-old Alfredo Hernandez, who had been shot in the head and stomach in the 5100 block of South Justine Street on September 25, 1991. Wiggins was taken to an interrogation room at Brighton Park headquarters, located at 3900 S. California Ave. This is an Area 3 police station on the city's South side where Jon Burge was the presiding detective commander. According to Wiggins's mother, Carolyn, he was brought to the interrogation room without a lawyer or adult present. He was then beaten with a 15-inch rod. Then the officers brought out a black box. Inside the box were electrical wires with round clips on the ends and a switch that unleashed an electrical current.

In 1993, Marcus Wiggins's mother filed a lawsuit against the City of Chicago. The lawsuit stated that Wiggins suffered from severe post-traumatic stress disorder because of the torture he had undergone at the police station. The lawsuit requested compensatory and punitive damages but did not specify an amount. LeRoy Martin and Jon Burge were named in the suit but were not accused of personally torturing Wiggins. Burge was a defendant because he had been the commander at the time of the arrest and had known of, or condoned, the alleged torture. Martin was named in the suit because, as a police superintendent, he was responsible for the policies, practices, and customs of the department. The suit also named Sergeants John Byrne and Fred Bonke, and Detectives James O'Brien, Anthony Maslanka, John Paladino, Kenneth Boudreau, and Michael Kill.

In the lawsuit, Marcus Wiggins described what had happened to him, "They started—my hands started burning, feeling like it was being burned. I was—I was shaking and my—and my jaws got tight and my eyes felt they went blank. It felt like I was spinning. It felt like my jaws was like—they was—I can't say the word. It felt like my jaws was sucking in. I felt like I was going to die."

Marcus Wiggins's conviction was thrown out by a juvenile court in 1993, and his lawsuit was settled for $95,000, paid for by the City of Chicago. Wiggins suffered severely after being tortured by these detectives. He met with a psychologist, Antonio Martinez, for five sessions, who concluded that Wiggins was exhibiting symptoms of PTSD, including "extreme nervousness, uncontrollable stuttering, assuming the fetal position, thumb-sucking, uncontrollable trembling of the hands, headaches, anger, tenseness, and hyperalertness." His mother said, "I'm suffering now, seeing what he's going through. They need to get punished for what they did."

Marcus Wiggins was arrested again in 1998 for the murder of Theopolis Teague. There were many errors and missing pieces of information in this case. On

February 27, 1998, Theopolis Teague was said to have been driving along 51st Street in Chicago with Segdrick Farley and Terrence Tyler. When his car came to a stop, Wiggins had supposedly backed into his car. There was no damage to the rear bumper of the car Wiggins had been driving, even though there was said to have been enough force to push Teague's car backwards. Segdrick Farley testified that the car Wiggins had been driving was maroon or burgundy, but Wiggins had never owned a maroon or burgundy car; his car was black. The crime had taken place early in the morning, so it was odd that both Farley and Tyler could not tell the difference between black and burgundy in the daylight. Kelly Stokes, who testified against Wiggins, owned a maroon car. Teague had then driven to the 5200 block of South Marshfield, where he parked his car and checked it for any damage. Allegedly, in his confession, Wiggins stated that he had approached the victim and asked, "What is up now?" Teague and the others took off running and Wiggins allegedly fired his gun, which supposedly wounded the victim. Segdrick Farley approached the victim who was lying in an alley. Farley said "Stutter" shot him and evidence at trial showed that "Stutter" was Wiggins's nickname. However, Farley told Wiggins's lawyer, Lana Johnson, that he knew Terrence Tyler as Stutter and did not know that was also a nickname for Wiggins. Marcus also never knew the victim, Teague, or Segdrick Farley.

There was a lack of evidence in this case. According to the documentary, *Heroes for a Semester*, the police had not responded to the car accident so it is difficult to know if a car accident had even taken place. Supposedly, there had been 13 shots fired, but no bullets had been found at the scene of the crime. According to the detectives, the weapon that had been used in the crime was a 9mm semiautomatic. It is odd that no bullets had been found at the scene and that there had been only 13 shots fired. It is also odd that the detectives were sure that was the gun which had been used, since the murder weapon was never found.

One of the people who testified against Wiggins, Kelly Stokes, owned a 9mm semiautomatic gun. The shots fired evidence was based on how many shots neighbors had heard. The police officers did not canvas the area properly and did not return to the scene to speak with neighbors they had missed. According to William Dorsch, retired homicide detective and current investigation expert, the preliminary report was written by the patrol officers and may not have been accurate. It would have been the detectives's job to conduct a more inclusive investigation, which they had not done.

The way Theopolis Teague's body had been recovered also raised questions because he had been wearing only a t-shirt and boxers. This was suspicious since he was murdered in the winter. Winter in Chicago usually means below freezing temperatures and a good amount of snow. So it was very suspicious that that would be all he was wearing. The detectives were called to the hospital where the victim had already been pronounced dead. There were witnesses at the hospital and the detectives acquired a name and pursued the defendant, Wiggins. Also, no bullet was ever recovered from Teague's body.

Three people testified against Wiggins: R.L. Mahan, Segdrick Farley, and Kelly Stokes. All three men later recanted, or expressed a desire to recant, their testimony. R.L. Mahan told Wiggins's ex-girlfriend, mother, and his own attorney that his testimony had been false. His original statement to the State's Attorney had been written for Mahan and all he had done was sign the document. In his testimony, Mahan said that Wiggins had said, "The rock boys hit my shit." This statement did not make sense because, according to this testimony, Wiggins was the one who backed his car into Teague's. On the day he was going to sign a document saying that he had lied in his testimony, Mahan was shot in the mouth and died as a result.

Segdrick Farley was harder to track down because he was, and is currently, serving time in Wisconsin. His testimony had been key to putting Wiggins behind bars. Farley had identified Wiggins in a lineup, after having been in police custody for 16 hours. He had been pressured by the police before he identified Wiggins as the shooter. Farley spoke with some of the makers of the documentary and said, "The police did Marcus wrong. The fucking identification was all fucked up." Farley was referring to having been shown Wiggins's photo before the lineup. The photo had also had Wiggins' name on it. He claims to have seen R.L. Mahan chase Teague into the alley. He had heard gunshots and then ran toward them. He said he had seen Mahan standing over Teague with a gun and then run into a getaway car. He said he had never seen Wiggins at the crime scene or in the car with Ladell Addams, R.L. Mahan, and Kelly Stokes.

The last witness was Kelly Stokes. In his original testimony he had claimed that Wiggins was a member of the Gangster Disciples. He was presented with an affidavit recanting his testimony, made sure it was accurate, and signed it. In this document he said Wiggins had never been a member of the Gangster Disciples, nor had he ever been involved with any gang. He also said he had been forced to testify against Wiggins by the homicide detectives.

There were many witnesses who Wiggins's attorney, Lana Johnson, could have called in his defense, but she chose not to. Wiggins's mother believes that Johnson thought there was enough evidence to prove Wiggins's innocence without having to call those witnesses. Alisha Wilson had been subpoenaed as a witness, but Wiggins's attorney did not put her on the witness list and she was not called to testify. Wilson has said she thinks that was not fair to Wiggins.

Wiggins's mechanic, Marcus Weatherby, was also supposed to testify on behalf of Wiggins but, sadly, passed away before the trial. Mr. Weatherby had told his wife about testifying since the black, four-door car in his possession had supposedly been used in a shooting. Mr. Weatherby knew that to be false because it was not working at all. Wiggins's mother came to Weatherby's wife, Latanya Bowen-Weatherby, after her husband passed, asking her to talk to Wiggins's attorney. Mrs. Weatherby said she did not know Wiggins, but did know that her husband had had his black, four-door car that had not been running for a few days, including February 27, 1998. Wiggins's attorney asked her for her husband's records, but all she had was her husband's written witness statement that Wiggins had brought his car to be fixed on February 23, 1998 and that he had not had the chance to work on it because the police had come and towed the car on the 27th. Wiggins's attorney then asked Mrs. Weatherby if she would come to court and testify about what she had seen, heard, and read. She agreed. She went to the court on the day of Wiggins's trial to testify but never received a call from Lana Johnson.

Tracey Ross also signed an affidavit about what she knew about Wiggins. She had known Wiggins since 1992, started dating him in 1995, and had their son in 1997. She said he was a very good father and was always there for the both of them. He did not like where they were living because when he went to see his son, guys would pick on him for not being in their gang or selling drugs for them. She said he was a sweet, caring, good-hearted person, not the cold-blooded killer they were making him out to be. In the time Ross had known Wiggins, he had never been a part of any gang. She also said that Wiggins did own a black four-door car but knows, for a fact, that it was not working on the day of the murder because he had walked to her house to see their son. He didn't normally walk around the neighborhood because he was scared after everything he had gone through. She had asked him where his car was and he told her he had gone to get it fixed.

On January 19, 2004, R.L. Mahan asked Ross how to get in touch with Wiggins's mother because he wanted to help Wiggins get out of jail for a crime he did not commit. He told her Wiggins was being framed and that he told his lawyer over the phone, and another one at the trial, that Wiggins did not kill anyone and was not even there. He said he had been scared and the police had told him to say Wiggins did it.

Malinda Chavers also signed an affidavit about what she knew about the case. Chavers had been sitting on her porch at 51st and Justine with LaVar Commador when Teague approached them looking worried. Teague was a member of the Blackstones and had said the other members of the gang were going to kill him. According to Chavers, she had walked away so Teague and Commador could talk but she was still in earshot of the conversation. Teague told Commador that he was a witness to the murder of a man named Johnski committed by other members of the Blackstones. He was fearful for his safety.

Marcus Wiggins believes, for a number of reasons, that he was being framed by the same detectives who were involved in his torture case years earlier. The detectives who tortured him in 1991 were very interested in his case. Wiggins claimed in his Post-Conviction Petition that James O'Brien, one of the detectives who had tortured him, and other detectives, made deals with, coerced, and threatened gang members to testify against him in court. O'Brien popped in the interrogation room where Wiggins was being held and told him to "go sit in a corner and suck your thumb because we are going to stick your ass with this one." Wiggins said that is when he knew he was being framed. During his interrogation, he told Detectives Gallegos, Riordan, and Omachi his alibi, where he had been, who he had been with, that his car had not been working at the time of the murder and he had left it with his mechanic to work on.

According to the documentary, *Heroes for a Semester*, Jane Raley, attorney with the Center on Wrongful Convictions at Northwestern, said that at the time of the murder Wiggins was living in Wisconsin so it was impossible for him to have committed the murder. He had witnesses willing to testify on his behalf, but Detective O'Brien and others threatened them. Police had also towed and destroyed his car prematurely, so that it could not be proven that it had not been involved in the crime or that it had not even moved. Wiggins also says that there was no physical evidence—no prints, no ballistics, no legitimate witnesses, nothing that could tie him to the murder of Theopolis Teague. He and many others do not even believe the murder took place on that street. He also believes there was no way he could have received a fair ruling under Judge Dennis Dernbach. Dernbach was a part of Jon Burge's go-to state's attorney team when extracting confessions under torture in 1984. He also claims the judge knew who he was and that he, O'Brien, and the state's attorneys conspired against him in court. .

Marcus Wiggins is currently incarcerated at Shawnee Correctional Center serving a 46-year sentence.

Jackie Wilson

On February 9, 1982, Detectives William Fahey and Richard O'Brien were killed during a traffic stop. The Chicago Police Department devoted hundreds of officers, working around the clock, and special funds allocated to finding the perpetrators. They knocked on doors and harassed and beat the largely Black population of the Chicago South Side neighborhood in the process. It was the largest manhunt in more than a decade.

At approximately 8:05 a.m. on February 14, 1982, Jackie Wilson was arrested for the murders of Officers Richard O'Brien and William Fahey and the armed robbery of the officers's service firearms. His brother, Andrew, had been arrested earlier that morning for the same crimes. Jackie Wilson was transported to Area 1 police headquarters. Sometime after 8:30 a.m., Area 2 Detectives Dennis McGuire, Lawrence Nitsche, Dale Riordan, and Thomas Krippel transported him to Area 2, where torturer Jon Burge was stationed, for interrogation by officers Thomas McKenna and Patrick O'Hara.

Detectives Nitsche and McGuire elbowed Jackie Wilson in the abdomen repeatedly during the car ride to Area 2 when he asked about the shootings, and Krippel slapped him. He was taken to a room with 12 to 16 plainclothes officers and hit in the head with a telephone book and was warned it would happen every time he lied. When Wilson declined to talk, he was hit with a book by about six officers as well as being poked and kicked. Another officer interrupted, and Wilson was read his rights. Around this time, he heard his brother yelling and feared he would suffer worse torture if he further declined to talk.

The officers continued to question and intermittently beat Wilson for another hour or two when they didn't like his answers. He was slapped, kicked in the groin, shaken, and had his hands twisted and stepped on. An unidentified officer held his service revolver in Wilson's mouth, while others held his arms back, and cocked and uncocked it repeatedly. O'Hara slapped Wilson and was told by McKenna not to injure his face. Once Wilson gave his confession, Detectives Nitsche and McGuire warned Wilson to give the Assistant State's Attorney Lawrence Hyman the same information or they would start all over. He initially refused to sign the court-reported statement and asked for a lawyer, at which point ASA Hyman left to contact Wilson's attorney, R. Frederic Soloman. O'Hara and McKenna returned, and O'Hara threatened to break Wilson's fingers if he didn't sign.

In 1982, Judge John Crowley heard testimony on the motion by Jackie Wilson's court-appointed public defender to suppress the confession. That motion was denied. In 1983, under Circuit Court Judge John Crowley, the Wilson brothers were each convicted on two counts of murder for the deaths of the Officers Fahey and

O'Brien and two counts of armed robbery for the taking of their service revolvers. In 1985, Jackie Wilson's case went back and forth between the Appellate and State Supreme Courts and was ultimately remanded for a new trial.

On September 30, 1987, the Appellate Court upheld Judge Crowley's finding that Jackie Wilson's confession was voluntary but reversed his conviction on the basis that he was entitled to be tried separately from his brother. He was retried in the spring of 1989 by Judge Michael Getty and was found guilty on one count of murder of O'Brien and the armed robbery of both officers. Wilson's attorney, Kenneth Jones, filed a petition for leave to appeal in 1994, but it was denied by the State Supreme Court. In 2011, Jackie Wilson filed a claim with the Torture Commission.

In 2015, the Commission concluded by a preponderance of evidence that there was sufficient evidence of torture to merit judicial review. Jackie Wilson is still vying for a new trial based on the torture he received at the hands of Burge and his men. Wilson is still incarcerated at Menard Correctional Center serving life without parole.

Afterword:
Carolyn Johnson's Story

The above accounts focus on the direct survivors of police torture in Chicago. The individual lives of these once young men have been ruined by the racist policing of Black and Brown bodies. But entwined with their stories are the broader social networks that have been disrupted, the families, the neighborhoods, the city. Though these men were originally tortured decades ago, their torture is ongoing as long as they remain behind bars. Their families and loved ones also continue to suffer long after the original injustices of the interrogation rooms and the courtroom railroads.

Carolyn Johnson's story is echoed by countless other cases of police torture. Carolyn Johnson is the mother of Marcus Wiggins, whose torture has been documented in this booklet. Carolyn and her family have suffered ever since Marcus was first arrested in 1991; he was only thirteen years old at the time. He was abused and tortured by the police until they received a confession. Carolyn took it upon herself to file a lawsuit to defend her son, and, two years later, Marcus was released. He himself has seen psychologists and has been diagnosed with depression, anxiety and severe PTSD—a normal response to the abuse and torture he suffered at the hands of police and other inmates. It was only a short while later that he would be framed for the murder of someone he did not know and be arrested, yet again.

The second time Marcus was arrested, five years after his initial release, Carolyn experienced panic attacks, nightmares, depression, PTSD, and finally suffered a nervous breakdown, which led to her being hospitalized for a week. Since then, she has continued to see a counselor and psychiatrist. Carolyn has said that every time she hears police sirens in the night, she wakes up in a panic, terrified her other children will be taken away from her. Still, Carolyn has found some relief in the arms of the church. When Marcus heard that his mom had experienced a nervous breakdown, he told her to start learning the Ten Commandments and to go to a church. Since she started going to church she has grown closer to God. She continues to keep herself busy: She has volunteered and worked at quite a few places. While at Rainbow Push Coalition, she was Vice President of the Parent Advisory Board and earned a plaque. Carolyn keeps herself busy. She currently works at a group home for mentally ill women. She intentionally takes the night shift there, to help her keep the nightmares at bay.

Carolyn says that it's by the grace of God she continues to get through the long days and even longer nights without Marcus. She also says she is walking by faith and not by sight and that she intends to keep fighting for her son's freedom. When asked what she would like to say about her experience she said: "Even though this happened to me, I never knew that the world was so cruel, and the justice system was so cruel. I don't trust the justice system. I didn't know it was so cruel. It took for it to knock on my door for me to know how cruel it was... It takes mothers, poor mothers, Black mothers, Hispanic mothers... to stand up and fight for their loved ones. And I praise all the mothers [that have gone through this], especially the ones that are fighting... I'm still walking in faith. I haven't given up on my son. It ain't over till the fat lady sings. It ain't over 'til God says it is. I'm walking by faith and not by sight."

As for Marcus himself, he has over twenty immediate family members that he cannot see. Carolyn has had over eight surgeries in the last twelve years, due to her physical health being degraded by her mental health. Marcus has been unable to help support his mother or family in those times. Now, he has spent over half his life in prison, including the entirety of his marriage and fatherhood. Marcus is currently being housed in Shawnee. The last time Carolyn was able to go out and see him was on his wedding anniversary in September of 2017. He earned a degree while incarcerated and continues to help other inmates until, hopefully, he can be released.

The details may vary, but the toll on other survivors's families has been just as harsh. Carolyn is a fighter who has joined the people's movement for justice, and, together with other surviving families, is demanding justice not just for her own son, but for sons and daughters everywhere. Survivors of police torture, abuse, and murder are linking arms in solidarity, demanding justice, fighting for community power, and control over the police.

Glossary

Affidavit - A signed and notarized statement made under oath.

Affirmed - The court of appeals has concluded that the lower court decision is correct and will stand as rendered by the lower court.

Amicus Curiae - Latin for "friend of the court." Advice formally offered to the court in a brief filed by an entity interested in, but not a party to, the case.

Appeal - A request made after a trial by a party that has lost on one or more issues that a higher court review the decision to determine if it was correct. To make such a request is "to appeal" or "to take an appeal." One who appeals is called the "appellant;" the other party is the "appellee."

Arraignment - Proceeding in which a criminal defendant is brought into court, told of the charges in an indictment or information, and asked to plead guilty or not guilty.

Bench Trial - Trial without a jury, in which the judge serves as the fact-finder.

Circumstantial Evidence - Evidence that relies on an inference to connect it to a conclusion of fact.

Concurrent Sentence - Prison terms for two or more offenses to be served at the same time, rather than one after the other.

Consecutive Sentence - Prison terms for two or more offenses to be served one after the other.

De Novo - Latin, meaning "anew." A trial de novo is a completely new trial. Appellate review de novo implies no deference to the trial judge's ruling.

Due Process - In criminal law, the constitutional guarantee that a defendant will receive a fair and impartial trial.

Evidentiary Hearing - Court proceeding prior to trial that involves witnesses giving testimony before a judge under oath.

Exclusionary Rule - Doctrine that says evidence obtained in violation of a criminal defendant's constitutional or statutory rights is not admissible at trial.

Exculpatory Evidence - Evidence indicating that a defendant did not commit the crime.

Habeas Corpus - Latin, meaning "you have the body." A writ of habeas corpus generally is a judicial order forcing law enforcement authorities to produce a prisoner they are holding, and to justify the prisoner's continued confinement.

Inculpatory Evidence - Evidence indicating that a defendant did commit the crime.

Mandatory Supervised Release - Formerly "parole," post-release period wherein parolee must adhere to certain terms and conditions set by a parole officer.

Motion - A request by a litigant to a judge for a decision on an issue relating to the case.

Motion in Limine - A pretrial motion requesting the court to prohibit the other side from presenting, or even referring to, evidence on matters said to be so highly prejudicial that no steps taken by the judge can prevent the jury from being unduly influenced.

Motion to Suppress - Motion filed to exclude statements based on the fact that the evidence they are seeking to suppress was obtained in violation of the defendant's constitutional rights.

OPS - Office of Professional Standards; was a department within the Chicago Police Department in which police investigated allegations of police misconduct.

Petition for Leave to Appeal - Document requesting permission to appeal the court's decision.

Post-Conviction Petition - Petition for post-conviction relief is an application to the court, filed by or on behalf of a person convicted of and sentenced for the commission of a criminal offense. It seeks to have the conviction or sentence set aside or an appeal granted on the ground or grounds that the conviction, or the sentence, or the denial of an appeal violated the state or federal constitution.

Preponderance of Evidence - A majority of the evidence.

Pro Se - Serving as one's own lawyer.

Public Defender - An attorney employed by the government on a full-time basis to provide legal defense to defendants who are unable to afford counsel.

Remanded - Sent back for new trial, as in a case being sent back to a lower court.

Reversal - A higher court setting aside the decision of a lower court. A reversal is often accompanied by a remand to the lower court for further proceedings.

Statute of Limitations - The time within which a lawsuit must be filed or a criminal prosecution begun. The deadline can vary, depending on the type of civil case involved or the crime charged.

TIRC (Illinois) - Illinois Torture Inquiry and Relief Commission; Illinois commission that investigates claims of torture by police, especially those perpetrated by former Chicago Police Commander Jon Burge and officers under his command.

Waiver of Rights - Signing a waiver of rights as part of a recorded statement means the signers are surrendering their right not to incriminate themselves, under the 5th Amendment of the U.S. Constitution.

Writ of Certiorari - An order a higher court issues in order to review the decision and proceedings in a lower court and determine whether there were any irregularities.

Resources

https://www.injusticewatch.org/news/2016/nicholas-ford-reversals-cook-county-judge

http://www.chicagotribune.com/news/ct-jon-burge-detective-accuser-seeks-justice-met-20150916-story.html

http://www.chicagotribune.com/news/local/breaking/ct-overturn-conviction-detective-testifies-met-20160119-story.html

https://www2.illinois.gov/sites/tirc/documents/case%20disposition%20clayborn%20smith.pdf

https://www.dnainfo.com/chicago/20130411/englewood/judge-expected-rule-on-alleged-torture-case-prosecuted-by-anita-alvarez

https://www.illinois.gov/tirc/documents/2015.7.22%20gibson%20disposition-stamped.pdf

https://www2.illinois.gov/sites/tirc/documents/2017.1.20%20deloney%20determination-stamped.pdf

http://www.illinoiscourts.gov/opinions/appellatecourt/2016/1stdistrict/1141109.pdf

https://www2.illinois.gov/sites/tirc/documents/case%20disposition%20scott%20mitchell.pdf

https://casetext.com/case/people-v-mitchell-1135

http://www.chicagotribune.com/news/ct-jon-burge-torture-cases-20130726-story.html

http://caselaw.findlaw.com/il-court-of-appeals/1527897.html

https://www2.illinois.gov/sites/tirc/documents/may%202015%20anderson%20order.pdf

https://www2.illinois.gov/sites/tirc/documents/case%20disposition%20tony%20anderson.pdf

http://articles.chicagotribune.com/1988-12-30/news/8802280476_1_michael-lynch-indictment-major-cocaine-dealer

https://www.leagle.com/decision/19891083185illapp3d8981972

http://peopleslawoffice.com/wp-content/uploads/2014/03/3.12.14j.biebelorder.pdf

https://www2.illinois.gov/sites/tirc/documents/case%20disposition%20kevin%20murray.pdf

https://www.rapsheets.org/illinois/doc-prisoner/fair_darrell/b32994

http://caselaw.findlaw.com/il-court-of-appeals/1731170.html

http://chicago.indymedia.org/archive/newswire/display/74747/index.php

http://chicago.indymedia.org/archive/newswire/display/43402/index.php

http://www.illinoiscourts.gov/opinions/appellatecourt/2016/1stdistrict/1140030.pdf

https://www.courtlistener.com/opinion/2094772/people-v-patterson/

https://www.courtlistener.com/opinion/2023671/people-v-cannon/?

https://www2.illinois.gov/sites/tirc/documents/2016-3-4-christian-appellate-opinion.pdf

https://www2.illinois.gov/sites/tirc/documents/randle%20amended%20disposition.pdf

http://www.illinoiscourts.gov/opinions/appellatecourt/2016/1stdistrict/1142125.pdf

http://www.chicagolawbulletin.com/archives/2016/11/28/cpd-torture-reopened-11-28-16

https://casetext.com/case/people-v-allen-752

http://illinoiscourts.gov/r23_orders/appellatecourt/2014/1stdistrict/1120209_r23.pdf

http://caselaw.findlaw.com/il-court-of-appeals/1188842.html

http://caselaw.findlaw.com/il-court-of-appeals/1730368.html

https://www.leagle.com/decision/20011007750ne2d25711002

https://www.leagle.com/decision/19931725620ne2d110511665

https://www2.illinois.gov/sites/tirc/documents/case%20disposition%20harvey%20allen.pdf

http://www.chicagotribune.com/news/local/breaking/ct-ivan-smith-torture-commission-met-20160125-story.html

https://chicago.suntimes.com/chicago-politics/burge-detectives-tortured-2-men-serving-life-terms-panel-says/

http://articles.chicagotribune.com/1991-08-09/news/9103270212_1_drive-by-shootings-wounds

https://www2.illinois.gov/sites/tirc/documents/2015.1.20%20i.%20smith%20determination%20stamped.pdf

https://www2.illinois.gov/sites/tirc/documents/2015.5.20%20ewilson%20determination%20appendix-stamped.pdf

http://caselaw.findlaw.com/us-7th-circuit/1180072.html

https://www.courtlistener.com/opinion/1985805/people-v-wilson/

https://www.courtlistener.com/opinion/2017036/people-v-wilson/

http://www.nytimes.com/1982/02/15/us/2-arrested-in-chicago-s-search-for-killers-of-police.html

http://articles.chicagotribune.com/1989-05-04/news/8904090802_1_jackie-wilson-chicago-police-officer-murders

http://articles.chicagotribune.com/1989-05-25/news/8902040225_1_jackie-wilson-police-officers-second-officer

http://articles.chicagotribune.com/1989-04-26/news/8904070454_1_jackie-wilson-andrew-wilson-chicago-police-officer

http://www.chicagotribune.com/news/local/breaking/ct-met-jon-burge-jackie-wilson-hearing-20171222-story.html

http://www.nytimes.com/1982/02/15/us/2-arrested-in-chicago-s-search-for-killers-of-police.html

https://www.alternet.org/story/104732/families_of_the_victims_tortured_by_chicago_detectives_rejoice_at_first_arrest

http://articles.chicagotribune.com/1993-01-14/news/9303161960_1_jon-burge-chicago-police-board-police-custody

https://casetext.com/case/us-v-lambert-13

https://www2.illinois.gov/sites/tirc/documents/case%20disposition%20robert%20smith.pdf

https://www2.illinois.gov/sites/tirc/documents/shawn%20whirl%20case%20disposition.pdf

https://www2.illinois.gov/sites/tirc/documents/reed%20amended%20determination%20without%20markup.pdf

https://www2.illinois.gov/sites/tirc/documents/2018.3.29%20johnson%20determination-stamped.pdf

The Chicago Alliance Against Racist and Political Repression

The Chicago Alliance Against Racist and Political Repression (CAARPR) was founded in 1973 as a local branch of the National Alliance, which grew out of the mass movement to Free Angela Davis and All Political Prisoners. The Chicago Alliance continues to struggle for justice with a focus on the following goals:

Establish Civilian Control of Police

From its inception, the CAARPR has campaigned against police crimes committed primarily against people of color and the poor. The Alliance initiated a campaign to Stop Police Crimes, especially passage of legislation to establish an elected Civilian Police Accountability Council that holds police officers accountable for crimes such as assault, murder, torture, and racial profiling. Victims of those crimes and their families are actively involved. This has become a mass movement that has placed this issue squarely on the agenda.

Stop All Police Torture of Suspects and Free All Survivors of Police Torture and Frame-ups

The Alliance has initiated a mass campaign to demand that the Governor grant all survivors of police torture unconditional pardons and free them from prison.

Free Political Prisoners and the Innocent

Working with mass progressive organizations, the Alliance has successfully campaigned for the release of many persons falsely charged and sentenced to death or to long prison terms.

End the Death Penalty

The U.S.A. has more people on death row than any other country in the world. The Alliance works with other organizations to end the death penalty. The abolition of the death penalty in Illinois has helped thrust this issue on the national agenda.

Abolish the "Other" Death Penalty

We oppose sentencing anyone to Life Without Possibility of Parole, or death in prison.

The Alliance works to fight racism, sexism, homophobia, anti-Semitism, anti-Islamism, immigrant bashing, religious discrimination, and all other forms of bigotry; to defend the rights of labor, especially the right to organize; to defend civil liberties; to expose and abolish the prison industrial complex, the "war on drugs," and the cradle to prison pipeline for people of color; to secure health care for prisoners; to support affirmative action; and to end systemic racism.

Chicago Alliance Against Racist and Political Repression

(312) 939-2750   caarpr.org

Membership Application

Please note: Membership is free for prisoners.

☐ Please sign me up as a member of the CAARPR.

    ☐ My annual dues of $15 are enclosed.

    ☐ I would like to pay in 3 installments of $5. The first $5 is enclosed.
(Dues installment dates are Jan. 1, May 1 and Sept. 1.)

☐ I would like to be a CAARPR Sustainer.

    ☐ Monthly Sustainer   ☐ Quarterly Sustainer

    ☐ $25 ☐ $35 ☐ $50 ☐ Other _____

☐ My contribution is enclosed. Contributions over $15 include membership.

    ☐ $35 ☐ $50 ☐ $100 ☐ Other _____

Name _____

Address_____

City _____

State _____ Zip _____

Phone _____

Email_____

Make checks out to: CAARPR

Mail to:
Chicago Alliance Against Racist and Political Repression
1325 S. Wabash Ave. Suite 105
Chicago, Illinois 60605